RELIGIOUS DOGMATICS

AND THE

EVOLUTION OF SOCIETIES

by
Niklas Luhmann

Translated with an introduction by
Peter Beyer

Studies in Religion and Society
Volume 9

The Edwin Mellen Press
New York and Toronto

Library of Congress Cataloging in Publication Data

Luhmann, Niklas.
    Religious dogmatics and the evolution of societies.

    (Studies in religion and society ; v. 9)
    Translation of: Religiöse Dogmatik und gesellschaft-
liche Funktion, which was published as chapter 2 of:
Funktion der Religion. 1977.
    Bibliography: p.
    Includes index.
    1. Religion and sociology. I. Title. II. Series:
Studies in religion and society (New York, N.Y.) ; v. 9.
BL60.L84   1984   306'.6   84-8976
ISBN 0-88946-866-4

Studies in Religion and Society
ISBN 0-88946-863-X

Copyright ©   1984, Niklas Luhmann

                   The Edwin Mellen Press
                       P.O. Box 450
                   Lewiston, New York 14092

          Printed in the United States of America

STUDIES IN RELIGION AND SOCIETY

INTRODUCTION

Although the sociological theories of Niklas Luhmann have been the subject of much discussion and even controversy on the European continent during the past fifteen years, they have received comparatively little attention in the English-speaking world. One of the important reasons for this state of affairs is undoubtedly that the translation of his more important works from the German has begun only recently.[1] The present volume attempts to contribute to the solution of this problem. It is a translation of "Religiöse Dogmatik und gesellschaftliche Evolution," one of Luhmann's major contributions to the sociology of religion. This work was first published in 1972 and again in 1977 in a significantly revised form.[2] The present translation is of this latter version.

The purpose of this introduction is threefold. First, since this work has been chosen with a view to introducing scholars, especially in the fields of religious studies and theology, to Luhmann's thought, some attempt must be made to mitigate the reader's initial unfamiliarity with new concepts, with new uses of seemingly familiar concepts, and with the ways that these concepts fit into Luhmann's overall theory of society. Second, *Religious Dogmatics and the Evolution of Societies* cannot be understood properly unless it is seen generally in the context of this overall theory of society and specifically in the context of Luhmann's overall theory of religion. The introduction responds to this requirement. Finally, Luhmann's thought is for the most part very complex and very abstract. This characteristic is attributable in part to the breadth of the theories

and in part to what may be called their non-linearity or
multi-dimensionality.   Because of this feature, it seems
advisable to introduce the reader to Luhmann's conceptual
grid.   Although this procedure necessitates a somewhat
lengthy journey through what is often very abstract and very
difficult territory, the attempt will allow a better orientation in what may otherwise seem like an opaque maze of
overly abstract categories.

       According to Luhmann, his theories are complex and
abstract because they are ambitious.[3]   He wishes to
construct a general theory that is descriptive and explanatory, from a sociological point of view, of all aspects of
modern day society and its predecessors.   This ambition
leads not only to complexity and abstraction, but also to
what Luhmann calls universal applicability and totalization.
By universal applicability he means no more than that the
theory can be applied to all social phenomena.   It does not,
for instance, restrict its statements to the realm of organizations, the realm of the family, of politics, or of
small, simple, and isolated societies.   However, universal
applicability does not imply that the theory can capture the
full concreteness of reality in its statements.   Because it
is abstract, the theory is also selective.   The ambition
towards totalization is also not as extreme as this word
might imply.   It refers simply to the aspiration of this
theory to account for all other theories of society within
itself.   This claim does not mean that Luhmann thinks he has
developed the ultimate theory of society.   It would be more
accurate to say that Luhmann believes his theory to be more
up to date.   It claims to be more reflective of modern society as it is in the late twentieth century.   For Luhmann,
any theory of society is a correlate of particular societal
structures.   His theory claims to supercede or totalize

other theories to the extent that these latter are reflective of past societal structures. Far from overcoming ideology, Luhmann's theory is rather an expression of its inescapability.

In order to get a clearer idea of what this sort of totalization might imply, one can consider Luhmann's relation to some of his predecessors and contemporaries. The most important of these, in terms of influence, is undoubtedly Talcott Parsons. Luhmann studied under Parsons in the early 1960's. The Parsonian influence is easily detected (and admitted) in most of his work. The most outstanding example is Luhmann's consistent and extensive reliance on functional systems theory both as a methodological and theoretical tool. Moreover, Luhmann divides his theory of society into three sub-theories: a theory of systems, a theory of evolution, and a theory of communication.[4] All three have roots in the Parsonian system. Many of the cornerstones of Luhmann's theory derive from Parsons. However, far from being one of dependency, Luhmann's relation to Parsons is one of development. Thus, for instance, Luhmann derives his important concept of communications media (see below, pp. xxxivff.) from the Parsonian concept of generalized media of interchange. These latter operate in the Parsonian system to relate the four principal subsystems of the four-function, AGIL paradigm.[5] Luhmann rejects the restriction to four principal societal functions imposed by the paradigm. He postulates his principal societal functions on the basis of what amounts to empirical observation and not from an abstract, generative model. It is the idea of such a generative model that Luhmann rejects. Without this derivation, his concept of communications media can float more freely and be developed more independently of the rest of the theoretical structures.[6] In general, Luhmann's

theory does not derive from a unified, axiomatic model. It
does not display such unity any more than the society in
which it is conceived.

The relation of Luhmannian theory to the phenomenological tradition, especially to Edmund Husserl, is similar
in that it takes up key phenomenological concerns and
achievements while developing them in such a way that phenomenological concepts will contribute appreciably to his own
theory and at the same time lose those features that Luhmann
sees as leading into difficulty. These features are again
traced to the presumed need for a unifying and axiomatic
starting point.

An example will make this relation clear. Luhmann's
concept of meaning uses the Husserlian idea of "horizon" to
express the fact that all meaning refers to many other possibilities that are not represented in the meaningful structure itself. That is, a symbol or object which means A
appears against a background of all that which is *not* A.
The undetermined not A's are the horizon of A, they are a
condition for the possibility of A. Luhmann lifts the concept of "horizon" from the Husserlian context of the intentionality of the transcendental subject and applies it to
his own concepts of personal and social systems. By doing
this, he hopes to avoid what he sees as Husserl's problems
with intersubjectivity while at the same time gaining a
clear analysis of the constitution of meaning and thereby,
of social structures and processes in general.[7] What is
important here is that Luhmann seeks to avoid certain theoretical problems by rejecting the unifying and axiomatic
starting point of the transcendental subject. For him, the
transcendental subject is a semantic correlate of structural
transformations in early modern European society. At the
time, it served to help that society through certain

critical transitional phases[8] and had its truth in that context. Today, it only masks the new socio-structural situation and therefore stands in the way of a more adequate theory of society.

The secondary literature on Luhmann's theory is extensive, at least in German.[9] The majority of this literature is critical. The critique fastens onto various aspects of Luhmann's theory, but there is a preponderance of such work that concentrates on the political implications of the theory and its character as ideology in the Marxian sense.[10] That is, the critique tries to show how Luhmann's theory is really a defense of existing power structures in our society, a defense in the guise of a supposedly objective theory. From what has been said thus far, it should not be surprising that Luhmann's response to this kind of critique is to accept it to the extent of admitting that his theoretical efforts are a reflection of existing societal structures and therefore ideological, but to reject the theoretical basis upon which the critique rests: namely, a certain vision of society.

Totalization, for Luhmann, implies, as it does for many of his critics, being able to explain the stance taken by those who oppose his theory within his own theory. In response to this demand, he meets the critique of scholars like Jürgen Habermas by comparing his theoretical output with what he subsumes under the rubric, "the humanistic tradition." A brief look at this comparison will not only give an idea of how Luhmann responds to the critique of his theory as ideology, but will also give more insight into the basic assumptions of his thought.

The fundamental contrast between Luhmann and those whom he sees as representing the humanistic tradition is that, for the former, society is not made up of human beings.[11]

Luhmann considers human beings, as individuals, to be part
of the environment of any social system. By contrast, social systems consist of communicative acts. Human individuals are personal as opposed to social systems. They are in
this theory a prerequisite for the existence of social systems, of which society is but one, but they are not subsystems of any social system. Only the communicative acts in
which human beings engage are included in the social systems. Luhmann's theory of society is therefore in this
sense impersonal.

The humanistic tradition then considers society to
consist of human beings. Luhmann believes that this conception has certain historical roots which tie it to the
structures of past societies and that it has certain unac-
ceptable consequences for the adequate understanding of
twentieth century societal structures. To begin, the humanistic conception is derived from a conception of human
beings, from an anthropology. The vision of society will
therefore be a direct derivative of the vision of the human
person. As for Husserl's transcendental subject, Luhmann
considers this way of looking at society to be a reflection
of a bygone socio-structural situation in European society.
Anthropology served as a substitute for a theory of society
at a time when the society was in a radical state of transition. Luhmann believes that today the situation is such
that a theory of society is once again possible and necessary for an adequate understanding of who we are.

The inadequacy that Luhmann sees in the humanistic
tradition can be made clearer by looking at the possible
consequences of the humanistic foundation of the idea of
society in anthropology. The conception of the human that
is of greatest interest here is one which sees it as
basically individualistic and founded on freedom and desire.

For such a view, society can only be justified to the extent
that it offers structures which enhance the opportunities
for humans to pursue their desires and act out their freedom. This view will tend to look at the society it is analyzing from a *negative* point of view. Any society will be
analyzed in terms of its repressive characteristics. A
theory, such as Luhmann's, which attempts a *positive*
description and explanation of that society will be seen as
one that justifies an order that is fundamentally unjust.
Luhmann therefore traces the opposition of especially the
critical theorists (viz. Habermas) to their conception of
the relation between human beings and society. According to
Luhmann, this negative stance can be overcome by his own
kind of theory, a functional systems theory that no longer
bases its concept of society on its concept of the human.
It can remain an open question here whether or not Luhmann
has grasped the logic of the humanistic position properly.
Be that as it may, it is worth noting that one of the human-
ists, Jurgen Habermas, has begun to lay the groundwork for a
theory of society which has a driving motive the emanci-
pation of human beings.[12]
    The foregoing is of course not a complete assessment of
the relation between Luhmann and his predecessors and
contemporaries. Such an assessment is far beyond the scope
of this introduction. What has been presented does however
indicate some of the epistemological assumptions upon which
the whole theory is based. This must be kept in mind when
reading the following work on religion. Luhmann's thought
is not founded on any metaphysical absolutes. Moreover, the
theory does not consider itself to be capable of judging the
possible validity of such absolutes.
    In addition, what has been said thus far shows that
Luhmann's theory cannot be seen simply as a continuation of

an existing theory, say that of Parsons. Nor is it merely a
combination of Parsonian systems theory with features of
Husserlian phenomenology. Luhmann's sociology is Parsonian
to some degree in its method (functional), in its
abstractness, and in its breadth. It is Husserlian to some
degree in its occasional use of phenomenological method and
in its radicalness. This latter term, in Luhmann's case,
means that he attempts to leave none of his foundational
concepts unanalyzed. Each of the core concepts, whether it
be system, function, reflection, meaning, selection, complexity, world, contingency, evolution, or communication, is
broken down into constituent relations and then recombined
with other concepts that determine the theory. The foundational concepts in Luhmann's theory are not just related to
one another, they are all mutually interdependent.

This feature of Luhmann's theoretical structure may be
called open-endedness. The theory does not begin with any a
priori concepts that do not depend logically on other concepts in the theory for their meaning. It is not built up
on a logical equivalent of, for instance, the transcendental
subject nor does it finally refer to the logical equivalent
for ultimate reality. Luhmann sees himself as breaking away
from what may be termed the Greek metaphysical tradition.[13]
Such fundamental and familiar concepts as substance and
being cease to operate in his theory. They are, if not
replaced, then displaced by concepts such as system and
complexity respectively. These latter concepts, which will
be examined in more detail later, are fundamentally different from the former in that they are relations. Whereas
substance is a unity of form and matter and being is the
primary predication of substance, complexity is closer to
being the relation between form and matter.[14] System, on
the other hand, is constituted as a system/environment rela-

tion so that system has no meaning without its environment and vice versa.

Open-endedness therefore implies the relativity or "relationality" and interdependence of all of Luhmann's foundational concepts. This fact makes presentation of the theory difficult. To start with the description of any one concept implies an understanding of at least some of the others. Husserl could start with the transcendental ego; Aquinas could start with God; Luhmann must always start in the middle because of the nature of his theory. This necessity can be seen in Luhmann's publications. None of these attempts a systematic presentation of the whole (the theory does not consist of parts). Certain key articles attempt to explain certain key concepts.[15] Other works develop the theory on the basis of the key concepts, devoting relatively little space to their elaboration. Even these latter works do not present a complete elaboration. Thus, *Funktion der Religion*[16] consists of five chapters, each of which is a study on its own. They can all be read separately and do not presuppose the reading of the others except insofar as all Luhmann's works presuppose many of the others. Anything like a complete sociology of religion is not attempted here or anywhere else.

These important features of Luhmann's theoretical style must be kept in mind when reading the work presented in this volume. Relatively little space is devoted to explaining concepts that are central to the arguments presented. To some degree, this introduction hopes to compensate for this lack. In what follows, we will examine many of the key concepts in Luhmann's conceptual grid. They are only presented in such detail as seems important for the understanding of the study that follows. A thorough consideration of the entire grid and all its interconnections is well beyond

the scope of a short introduction and is in any case something that Luhmann himself has not undertaken.

An understanding of Luhmann's concept of system can
begin by distinguishing it from other concepts of system.[17]
The first of these sees a system as a whole made up of
parts. The order of the parts guarantees the continued
existence of the whole. Such a concept refers purely to an
internal order: it is defined without reference to an environment. A second concept takes the environment into consideration, but only as a potential threat to the system. The
environment is not seen as constitutive for the system. A
concept that comes closer to Luhmann's sees system and environment as interdependent. In this view, a system selectively processes input from the environment and responds by
changing its state or attempting to influence the
environment with selective outputs. The system then is a
combination of processes that maintains itself by maintaining a boundary between itself and the environment. The
concept of system that Luhmann uses carries this idea to a
higher level of abstraction by defining the difference
between system and environment as a difference in complexity. The environment is always more complex than the system: that is, there are always more possibilities in the
environment than in the system. However, there must be
enough possibilities in the system to respond to the variety
of possible inputs from the environment.[18] Maintaining this
what Luhmann calls a complexity gradient between system and
environment constitutes the system as system. The strategies by which a system can use relatively few responses to
compensate relatively many environmental inputs constitute
the system's *selectivity*. The capacity for reducing
complexity is the selectivity of the system.

This idea of system, as described thus far, is still

extremely abstract. It is however necessary to begin at such a level to avoid the conception in the reader's mind that when Luhmann speaks of systems, he is referring to some concrete whole like a church or a political party. A better understanding of what systems are will be gained as we proceed to discuss some of the other central concepts.

The particular subset of systems with which Luhmann deals most often is that of social systems. These distinguish themselves from most other kinds of system in that their strategies for reducing complexity are based on meaning.[19] Another important type of system that is so based is the psychic or personal system. However Luhmann devotes relatively little space in his writings to this admittedly important type.[20] Examples of social systems are face-to-face interaction, organizations, and society with all its subsystems such as the religious system, social strata, the political system, etc. All these are based on meaning. This is therefore a concept of central importance for the entire theory.

Meaning is what gives form to social experience and action. Luhmann draws an analogy between the place of meaning in social systems and the place of RNA/DNA in organic systems.[21] In this sense, meaning is a code for experience and action. It gives experience and action a structure in terms of which these can be recognized as experience and action and can vary or be varied. Meaning is basic to social systems: social systems build up their selectivity through the use of meaning. Therefore, in the context of social systems, there cannot be such a thing as meaninglessness since the recognition of meaninglessness would already presuppose some meaning in terms of which this meaninglessness could be recognized. Moreover, in this Luhmannian concept, meaning cannot appear without reference

to systems that constitute it. Again we meet the open-endedness that excludes an ultimate and presuppositionless
referent.

Luhmann analyzes the particular way in which meaning
processes experience and action under the conceptual head-
ings of negation, generalization, and reflexivity. Just as
a system is identified through a system/environment relation, so for him is meaning constituted through a
determinate/indeterminate relation. A meaningful determination, that is, any particular meaningful thing, is constituted only in relation to the general host of other possible
determinations that are excluded in this particular case and
are therefore indeterminate.   The familiar figure/ground
relation from Gestalt psychology is very similar.   The
figure can stand out and be recognized only because there is
a background against which it can profile itself. The background is (necessarily!) perceptually vague, yet essential
if the specific figure is to be perceived at all.   Similarly, in Luhmann's terms, every meaningful determination
implies a generally indeterminate background of other possible determinations. This setting aside, leaving indeterminate, putting into the background, is what Luhmann means
by *negation*. The other possibilities are negated so that a
particular meaning may be posited. This negation operates
by generalizing these other possibilities.   The generalization functions to allow the negation in each case to be
inclusive of *all* other possibilities.

Furthermore, the generalization is not only operative
in terms of the negation. The given meaningful determination is generalized *along with* the indeterminate other
possibilities as a presupposition for the entire operation.
Thus, Luhmann can say that, for meaning, reality is modally
generalized.[22] In order to understand what this means, one

must look at what Luhmann calls the reflexivity of negation. The negation can itself be negated. It can be applied to itself. Any of the possibilities that are generally negated for the sake of a given meaningful determination can be brought out of their negated state and actualized, that is, made determinate. Similarly, a given figure can recede into the background in order that a new figure, which was initially part of the background, can be perceived. The reflexivity of negation means that the negated possibilities can become actualities in spite of having been negated. It is important to realize that, for Luhmann, negation is not radical. Negating a possibility does not imply that it is gone for good. Negation merely implies putting aside. The modality that is referred to in modal generalization is that of possible/actual. The generalization refers to the interchangeability of the actual and the possible. It is worth noting that Luhmann only goes so far as to say that meaning presupposes the modal generalization of reality; he does not say "modes of being." This expression would presumably be getting too close to a substantive view of reality and is accordingly avoided. Luhmann maintains the open-endedness of his theory by replacing unities with relations.

Having defined meaning in this way, he can say that meaning forces selectivity on experience and action.[23] Since meaning is here the form for experience and action and since this form operates only with reference to other possibilities, experience and action in social systems must appear as selections from among many possibilities. As the foundation of a social system's selectivity, meaning structures the world of both the possible and the actual, and this both within the system and in the environment. It constitutes the complexity of the system and the environment (i.e., the world) such that the selectivity of experience

and action can constitute the system vis-a-vis its environment.

The examination of the place of meaning in Luhmann's
theory leads to a consideration of what is meant by the term
complexity.[24]   As has been the case with the other major
concepts considered thus far, complexity is a word that
seems familiar but whose denotation shifts in this theory.

It will be sufficient for our introductory purposes to
understand the connection between complexity and selectivity.   These terms must be seen as interdependent if the
former is not to appear as the a priori that Luhmann seeks
to avoid.   We have seen that a system is determined as a
relation to its environment.   This relation is described as
a complexity gradient, indicating the relation of a more
complex environment and a less complex system.   We have also
seen that the reduction of complexity involved in this asymmetrical relation constitutes the system's selectivity.   In
Luhmann's view, this selectivity is not simply a one-way
street.   The selectivity of systems, that is, the fact that
their order is created by a selection from many possibilities, also constitutes the complexity that it reduces.   In
this statement can be seen the radicalness of the statement
by Luhmann that systems *realize and reduce* complexity.[25]
This idea can be illustrated with the concept of meaning
just discussed.   Meaning is constituted by systems: that
is, there is no meaning without systems.   It is only in the
light of a given meaningful determination that the indeterminate, "appresented" possibilities appear as represent*able*
possibilities.   The meaning constituting process itself
gives the field from which selections are made its character
as "appresented" horizon.[26]

Given that selectivity and complexity thus mutually
determine each other, Luhmann can logically conclude that

environmental complexity is also constituted through systemic processes of selection. Just as the system must have its own internal complexity correspond to the complexity of its environment in order that the system may establish and maintain itself, so the environmental complexity, for the system, varies with the complexity of the system. The environment is not a constant in terms of complexity. Being interdependent with the system, Luhmann sees it as variable. Put in somewhat oversimplified language, the system sees its environment in terms of itself. The more complex the system, the more complex will its environment be seen. Thus, for example, a simple society, as an example of a (social) system, will not have an environment that is as complex as the environment of modern society because the simple society is itself internally less complex than its modern counterpart. In Luhmann's sociology of religion, this mutual correspondence of systemic and environmental complexity becomes important for the religious system of modern society. Not only is there pressure for the religious system to adjust its own internal complexity to the increased complexity of the (especially: inner-societal) environment, but there is also an obverse pressure for the religious system to reconstitute or re-envision its environment, and this in *religious* terms. It is not simply a question of accommodation by religion to modern society; it is also a question of reformulating the complete system/environment relation from the perspective of religion. It is on this basis that Luhmann can question the adequacy of continued reinterpretation of the received religious traditions as the foundation of the task of theology in today's society. In the work introduced here, Luhmann suggests that, in addition, theology may find it advisable to proceed more self-consciously in terms of religion's social nature (i.e.,

its function) and less on a basis that considers this aspect
of the religious task to be self-evident.[27]

This idea of the correspondence of system and environment complexity immediately raises the question of
Luhmann's definition of complexity. As might be expected,
Luhmann defines complexity as a relation. Roughly, complexity is here the relation between the range of possibilities and the reductive strategies that structure the
access to these possibilities. Within a system, complexity
is the relation between those elements that make up the
system and the structurally permitted relations between
these elements. This definition can perhaps be understood
better if one concentrates on the relation between complexity and selectivity. An increase in the number of elements
(possible experiences and actions) and in the number of
relations between these elements does not, on Luhmann's
definition, by itself mean increased complexity. This
obtains only if, in addition to the increase in elements and
relations, the system can also select its action and experience on the basis of this increase. In short, increased
complexity implies increased selectivity. Reducing *more*
complexity means *more* reduction, not only in the sense of
more structure, more reductive strategies, but also in the
sense of more *powerful* reductive strategies, ones which
eliminate more possibilities.

Two examples may assist further in understanding this
central idea. In spite of the increased possibilities in
terms of permitted behaviors in modern society and the
increase in the number of and relation between legal rules
that help to regulate such behavior, a judge in our society
can still come to definite decisions with regard to the
cases before him, and this on the basis of the increased
possibilities and relations. Analogously, taking an example

from a different era and a different domain, a priest in
late medieval European society could decide as to the guilt
of those who confessed to him and as to the form of peni-
tence for the sins in spite of the increase in possibilities
and circumstances of the sinful behavior attendant upon such
ideas as conscience and intention, the latter themselves
correlatives of structural changes in the society that
Luhmann estimates signalled an increase in societal complexity.[28]

    The correspondence of increased complexity and
increased selectivity has important consequences for
Luhmann's theory other than those already mentioned. Among
these is that increased selectivity, because it must eliminate more possibilities with one stroke, increases the
visible contingency of selective structures. The larger
number of excluded possibilities reveals to a greater extent
how the selection could have transpired otherwise. This
result will be seen to have important consequences for a
religious system that seeks to become more complex in a more
complex social world. It also brings us to Luhmann's concept of contingency, the obverse of complexity.

    Although systems constitute complexity through their
selectivity, one cannot conclude from this statement that
Luhmann is following strictly in the German idealist tradition. Like Parsons,[29] Luhmann wishes to do justice to the
fundamental insights of this tradition without succumbing to
its one-sidedness. Accordingly, the concept of complexity
has an obverse in the concept of *contingency*. He uses these
two concepts almost as a double concept, often substituting
one for the other in the same phrase.[30] This becomes
understandable when one looks at how he sees the two concepts. Complexity is constituted by the selectivity of
systems and selectivity implies both selection and a field

from which the selection is made. This field is for Luhmann
the field of other possibilities which are implied in every
selection as in the case of meaning. Complexity therefore
implies selection that could have transpired otherwise:
another possibility could always have been selected. The
concept of contingency expresses this "always-possible-
otherwise". For Luhmann, contingency means not only
non-necessity, but also substitutability. Since this definition of contingency makes of this concept simply another way
of looking at the syndrome of possible/actual and selectivity, every affirmation of contingency points to complexity and vice-versa. Hence, their interchangeability.

The idea of contingency makes Luhmannian complexity a
concept that includes the notion of risk. All selection is
risky because it negates other possibilities, that is, it
simplifies reality. Such simplification can lead to a situation in which the expectations surrounding a selection are
not met, are disappointed: the rainy season does not bring
the usual rains, a mother does not behave like a mother,
governmental policy does not bring prosperity, etc. This
aspect reveals the "realistic" strain in Luhmann's concept
of complexity. Selection cannot be carried out arbitrarily
because the world includes certain *constraints*, certain
barriers to variation. What precisely these barriers are,
Luhmann does not say, indeed on the basis of his theory, he
cannot say. Two consequences of this limitation are that
Luhmann does not claim that one can predict the future on
the basis of his theory of society, and that this theory
restricts the strictly scientific domain to exclude
questions about what society and human life ultimately
should be. He thereby leaves open a wide domain for, among
other things, religion and art, and cannot easily be accused
of scientific reductionism. However, it can also be argued

that, given this more or less positivistic scientific position, Luhmann does not face the question of how his theory
will be used politically and economically in concrete
society.

Be that as it may, for the present purposes, it is
enough to know that the concepts of complexity/contingency
and selectivity imply such constraints since otherwise,
there would be no change, no interest of the system in its
environment.[31] Risk as potential for failure is fundamental
to Luhmannian theory since systems presuppose this risk.
This idea can be formulated in terms of the system's function. Following Luhmann's idea of function, the function of
a system must be a relation between the system and some
problem of reference.[32] This problem appears in his concept
of world. The world for Luhmann is the totality of all
possibilities within and without the system, in the system
and in its environment. The world is a problem from the
point of view of its complexity. In order for the system to
emerge and sustain itself, it must reduce (and constitute)
this complexity. The function of a system, of its structures and processes, is to reduce the higher complexity of
the world. That feature of complexity which forces a system
to reduce complexity is indicated in the idea of the riski-
ness of all selection. That feature of a system which results in the constitution of complexity is indicated in the
idea of selectivity. Here again, in the concept of
complexity/contingency, we meet the open-endedness of
Luhmannian theory, its radical relativity, or better, "relationality".

In the context of Luhmann's sociology of religion, one
important thing that follows from this relation of the system to the world through complexity is that the world cannot
be transcended. Since the world is the totality of all

possibilities both in the system and in its environment,
selection must always be from among these possibilities.
All additional possibilities would by definition also belong
to the world. The world is the ultimate horizon of all
selectivity. Transcendence of this horizon would, as the
image of horizon implies, only shift the horizon, not go
beyond it.

A further Luhmannian concept of great importance in the
present context is that of *self-reference*. Under this
heading, he distinguishes three types: reflexivity, reflection, and fundamental self-reference. Luhmann rejects the
restriction of these concepts to the thinking about thinking, that is, to the mental processes of the thinking subject. Thus, reflexivity is defined as the application of a
process to itself or to something very similar to itself.[33]
An example of such reflexivity was met in the above discussion on meaning. There I spoke of the negation of negation.
Self-reference is a generalization of the basic idea involved in reflexivity as a subjective thinking about thinking.

Before turning our attention to the Luhmannian definition of reflection, we must first examine the idea of
fundamental self-reference. As a generalized concept,
self-reference applies not only to human beings but also to
other systems such as biological systems. The concept attains an objective reference here instead of just a subjective one. Self-reference is for Luhmann a basic feature
of systems. Accordingly, he sees social systems as being
constituted by communicative actions; but these
communications always refer to other communications. Within
social systems, all actions are related to all other actions. Since, for Luhmann, action is the word used when a
selection is attributed to the system as opposed to the

environment (experience), fundamental self-reference means
that all selections are related to other selections in the
system. This self-referential feature of especially social
systems is the basis for the construction of systems and of
their distinction from the environment.[34] Social systems
are for Luhmann self-referential in all their structures and
processes because they are founded on meaning. Meaning is
always self-referential: meaning is only meaningful with
reference to other meaning. Every operation within a social
system refers to other operations within this system.
Social systems are in this sense closed, but it is precisely
this closure that allows them to have contact with their
environment.

The circularity of meaning, that is, the fact that
social systems in this theory are based on self-reference,
allows the establishment of the system vis-a-vis the environment because it breaks the one to one correspondence
between system and environment. If such correspondence were
allowed to persist, then every input from the environment
would have a corresponding response in the system. There
would be no difference in complexity: every possibility in
the environment would have a corresponding possibility in
the system. Self-reference, for Luhmann, breaks this correspondence because each environmental input can be responded
to in the system only in terms of the self-referential,
meaningful structures. Put in a slightly different way,
social systems establish themselves with respect to their
environment because they react to everything only in their
own terms. Only meaningful occurrences in the world are
recognized.

The fundamental self-reference of the structure of
social systems also allows these to build an identity. Even
though the meaningful structures of systems can be changed

in response to their interaction with the environment, there
will always be aspects of this self-referential structure
that will remain constant, at least temporarily. These
constant aspects can be reflected as the identity of the
system. When a system turns its attention to its identity,
Luhmann speaks of reflection. Reflection is defined as the
relation of the system to itself.

Self-reference is basic to Luhmann's theory. It provides the basis upon which system/environment distinctions
can be built up, changed, and maintained. And since the
system/environment relation is the basis of complexity and
selectivity, the concept of self-reference is crucial to an
understanding of Luhmann's overall theory. In addition,
Luhmann considers self-referential structures to be a defining feature of modern society.[35] That is, the increased
dominance of these is seen as an important way by which
modern society is distinguished from its predecessors. This
aspect of the Luhmannian position determines to some extent
the kind of question he poses to modern-day religion and
modern-day theologians.

Given the fundamental position of the system as the
foundation of selectivity in Luhmann's theory, it is not
surprising to find that the concept of system *differentiation* plays a fundamental role as well. In the context of
systems, Luhmann defines differentiation as the repetition
of the system-building strategy within the system. Inasmuch
as a system constitutes its selectivity through the establishment of the system/environment boundary, so differentiation creates subsystems within the system to intensify the
selectivity of the system. Differentiation is a reflexive
strategy that, like all such strategies, allows a system to
make increasingly improbable selections. How is this so?
In a differentiated social system, specifically, in a differ-

entiated society, the communications relevant in one subsystem need not become directly relevant in the other subsystems because the subsystems are relatively independent of
one another. There is therefore a host of such communications that any given subsystem need not take into direct
consideration when selecting its own action. Occurrences in
the world, whether in the environment, the particular subsystem, or the rest of society, do not have to be accommodated in all sectors of the society in the same way. Any
subsystem of a society can depend on a more domesticated
inner-societal environment to handle certain problems before
they become problems for the particular subsystem. As a
simple example, the construction of a good highway is a
condition for the possibility of travelling 120km./hr. in an
automobile. Such selection on the part of the transpor-
tation system is at best relatively improbable in the
absence of such a domesticated, inner-systemic structure,
that is, in the absence of the internal differentiation into
road system and automobile system.

Returning to societal systems, Luhmann considers that
the advantages of differentiation work themselves out differently, depending on the type of differentiation.[36] He sees
three of these: segmentary, stratified, and functional.
Segmentary differentiation divides a system into many equal
subsystems. There is relatively little interdependence
among these subsystems. The destruction of one subsystem
does not destroy the entire system but only that subsystem.
Among societies, simple or primitive societies are seen to
show a primacy of segmentary differentiation. The division
into subsystems in such societies is based on descent or
settlement. The subsystems are equal in the sense that,
although a particular clan or village may be better off or
experience more prestige than another, such facts are at

least in principle accidental and do not spring out of the
structure of the society. If one clan or village is
destroyed by war or disaster, the others do not break up on
that account. The goings-on in one subsystem are not automatically relevant in all the others. And yet, together,
the various segments still form a society through economic,
political, familial, etc. interchanges. Each segment is not
communicatively isolated and self-sufficient.

     Although Luhmann bases his analysis of segmentary dif-
ferentiation and functional differentiation (see below) on
the Durkheimian distinction between mechanical and organic
solidarity, the addition of stratified differentiation
breaks with Durkheim and the entire segment of sociological
tradition that works with only two fundamental types of
social organization. For Luhmann, stratified differentiation differs from segmentary differentiation in that the
subsystems in the former are divided on the basis of *inequality*. The foundation of inequality between the subsystems of
a stratified society, that is between the social strata, is
an unequal distribution of wealth and power. Luhmann calls
this an unequal distribution of communication potential
since wealth and power are for him forms of communication.[37]
A further important characteristic of stratified societies
is that, within the subsystems, the basis of relation is
communicative equality. The members of the different strata
are considered in principle equal within their respective
strata. Luhmann sees one of the great advantages of
stratified societies over against segmented societies in
that the former can respond to the needs of larger and more
complex societies. When interaction among all members of a
society becomes unworkable, stratification allows the division into groups of communicative equals without thereby
eliminating the greater differentiation of roles that is

possible with the increased size and complexity. It intensifies selectivity in that selective communication is still
possible even though many more possible communications are
negated or disallowed. In other words, stratification allows a segment to become much larger and much more complex.
It offers a functional equivalent to renewed segmentation.
Moreover, the inequality between strata is maintained by
communication barriers. This feature allows, for instance,
differences in the religious outlooks and religious
practices of the various strata.

Luhmann sees modern society as one showing a dominance
of functional differentiation. This form creates societal
subsystems by allocating social communication to spheres,
each of which fulfills certain functions for the society as
a whole. Each of these major functions is vital for society
and no one of them can claim absolute priority. Examples of
these functions, as Luhmann analyzes them, are the political
function of providing collectively binding decisions, the
economic function of satisfying present and future needs,
and the religious function of managing the inevitability of
contingency. Luhmann's view of the development of functional subsystems for modern society is instructive of how
they are seen to operate. Already in earlier types of society, one finds a differentiation of roles such as merchant,
priest, or ruler, and of specific situations in which these
roles operate. He claims that the development of these
functional spheres into functional subsystems is dependent
on, among other things, the differentiation of other roles
that are complementary to the major roles that already
represent the functional spheres. Thus we have the producer
and the consumer, the cleric and the layman, the politician
and the public, or, to take examples from other subsystems,
teacher and pupil, doctor and patient. The communicative

relation of these complementary roles is seen by Luhmann as
asymmetrical. The first member of each pair is considered
to be the professional, the one who in a larger sense, represents the functional sphere in question. This professional-
ism is expressed in that the second member of each pair
usually accepts the communicative offering of the first to
the extent that it situates itself within the functional
sphere in question. Moreover, communication in functional
spheres crystallizes around specific binary schemata in
which the one term is more or less simply the negation of
the other. Examples are not having/having, suffering/salva-
tion (or sin/grace), uneducated/educated, and sick/healthy.

Functional subsystems are for Luhmann both equal and
unequal. They are unequal in that each fulfills a different
function. They are equal in that everyone, at least in
principle, has equal access to them. This, of course, does
not mean that there is no more unequal distribution of
communicative opportunities under a dominance of functional
differentiation. However, such inequality no longer, according to Luhmann, follows from the primary structure of the
society as it does in stratified societies. The way that he
expresses this is to say that access to one function is no
longer structurally dependent on the relation to other functions. In fact, Luhmann considers that functional differentiation is the fundamental structural correlate of the
modern semantic ideal of the equality of all human beings.[38]

Functional differentiation offers further intensification of selectivity in that the criteria of success in each
subsystem are relatively independent of the others. An
economic enterprise concerns itself mainly with economic
viability and much less with political implications, moral
rectitude, health, and education, except insofar as these
affect economic success. The political system is to a large

degree spared the necessity of being economically viable or
of asking ultimate questions about the nature of the world.
The political system must, however, consider its actions in
the light of political viability. Bankruptcy and electoral
defeat are for Luhmann parallel occurrences in the economic
and political systems.

This analysis must deal with a great number of characteristics of modern society that seem to belie the primacy
of such functional differentiation. Luhmann approaches this
task from various angles. Among these is an analysis of
what is meant by primacy. The theory postulates that all
three types of differentiation are present in all societies.
Thus, primitive societies exhibit a certain amount of functional role differentiation and a certain amount of stratification, both especially on the basis of sex, age, relation,
and achievement. Yet these two other types of differentiation operate within the context of the primary segmentary
differentiation. The primary identification of a person of
a given society is her/his tribe, clan, settlement community, etc. Only within the context of this determination do
the others operate.

Similarly, in traditional societies with a primacy of
stratification, functional and segmentary differentiation
are also present. Political and religious functional
spheres are often especially well developed. And societies
are often divided into political segments such as regions or
countries. Above all, each stratum is fundamentally segmented into the constituent families or lineages. Here
again, the secondary forms of differentiation operate within
the context of the primary form and support it.

Finally, in modern society, Luhmann sees both segmentary and stratified differentiation playing important structural roles. Above all, the economic system still relies on

stratification to order the relation of persons of the society to the production process. Moreover, segmentation in
above all the political and religious systems plays an important role in specifying these functional domains for diverse
life-situations. Nevertheless, Luhmann considers that it is
the overarching functional structures that give what he
calls modern global society its character as a single
society.

One of the consequences of the increased selectivity
brought by the primacy of functional differentiation is for
Luhmann that the subsystems can produce more possibilities
for the society than the society as a whole can actualize.
A typical example is the economic possibility of increasing
the chances of success of a business enterprise by "buying"
the   cooperation   of   politicians.   Such   an   economic
possibility can create serious problems in the political
system. Luhmann, in the work that follows, gives an example
from medieval theology (the beginnings of a differentiated
religious system) in which the religious possibility of
wishing the death of one's own father because it is God's
will was not a possibility for the family and therefore not
for the society as a whole.[39]

This overproduction of possibilities points to another
aspect of functional differentiation as Luhmann sees it.
Functional subsystems are interdependent. Because each of
them concentrates on one primary function, they must presuppose the fulfillment of other vital functions as a condition
for the possibility of their own autonomy and functioning.
The relation among subsystems leads to a consideration of
how the fulfillment of the primary functions is affected by
the existence of other functional subsystems in the inner-societal environment of any given one of them.

To approach this question, Luhmann distinguishes three

different relations that a subsystem of any society can
have. A subsystem can relate to the society as a whole and
does so on the basis of its function. A subsystem can
relate to the other subsystems of the society and does so on
the basis of what Luhmann calls performance. Finally, a
subsystem can have a relation to itself. From what was said
above, it is not surprising to see Luhmann refer to this
relation as reflection.[40]

These basic orientations are unavoidable once subsystems have been formed. However, the difficulty with which
all three relations are accommodated in subsystems depends
on the type of primary differentiation of a society. Thus
all three orientations are virtually identical in segmentary
societies since the society can be seen as a large version
of the subsystem. In stratified societies, hierarchical
structure and semantic correlates (ideologies) such as, in
Western society of the middle ages, the combination of the
ideas of means/end and whole/part, form the basis for conceiving these relations. Thus the upper strata can be seen
as the part that represents the whole and that embodies the
end of society. The relation to society and the relation to
self are thus the same. The relation of the upper strata to
the other subsystems is also on the basis of this hierarchical conception.

When Luhmann comes to analyzing modern societies, he
sees that, for each functional subsystem, including
religion, the three relations can interfere with each other.
The function can only be fulfilled to the extent that performance for the other subsystems is adequate. This results
from the interdependency of the subsystems. Luhmann gives
an example from the political system. This system, as has
been mentioned, provides binding decisions for the society.
In order to do this it must take care to ensure that it has

the support of the other subsystems. It must take into
account economic interests, family interests, health interests, educational interests, and perhaps religious interests, among others. All these interests represent the other
functional spheres of society and their particular needs.
However, balancing all these interests for the common good
and to maintain political power through the acceptance of
political decisions can lead to numerous issues that are
more or less undecidable.

The reflection relation, for Luhmann, becomes a problem
in a society that changes more or less rapidly. Identity,
as we have seen, implies continuity in the process of
change. Modern functionally differentiated society tends to
change repidly because, among other factors, the greater
selectivity of this society increases the visible contingency of all structures and processes. When rapid change
threatens continuity, reflection can become a problem. The
basis for action by a self-referential system in an environment, its identity, is thus threatened.

These, for Luhmann, are possible problems for the functional subsystems of modern society. He does not however
see them as problems that affect all functional spheres
equally. Functional differentiation into subsystems has a
selective impact on different functional spheres. Some of
these thrive more under this regime than others; some suffer
and experience more crises than others. It is in this context that this Luhmannian analysis of differentiation
becomes important for the analysis of religion.

As has been mentioned, the function of religion in this
theory is to manage the inevitability of contingency. More
precisely, Luhmann sees the central function of religion to
be the taming of the problem that all determinations, and
therefore all social determinations, are risky and to some

extent therefore, indeterminate, even indeterminable. Religion is inspired by the simultaneity of determinacy and indeterminacy, by the necessity of contingency. Yet the truly religious task is to go beyond the form of the problem to find a reason for this state of affairs in a sacred or holy realm beyond contingency.[41]

Luhmann therefore locates the function of religion at a very fundamental level of social structure. It operates very much on the level of the society as a whole. This location makes understandable why religion has been considered to have such overall relevance for all social experience and action in most societies in history. This centrality has made it seem reasonable to believe that religion is that which ultimately integrates any society. Such a conception of the relation of religion and society, whether by members of a society or by sociologists, did not have to face any serious challenges as long as function was not the dominant criterion for societal differentiation. In segmentary and stratified societies, the religious sphere and religious communication could cut across the respectively dominant lines of differentiation without serious challenge. However, on the Luhmannian model, in modern society, the shift in type of primary differentiation tends to relegate religion to the rank of just one functional subsystem among others. As has been pointed out, each major subsystem in modern society operates with reference to its own specific rationality or set of values: economic viability and political possibility were cited as examples. These specific rationales, centered around specific binary schemata, form the bases of the relative autonomy of the functional subsystems. Religion can no longer claim to found these other rationales except in a very transferred sense, and especially religious structures such as churches cannot easily

claim to dictate in these other spheres. Nevertheless,
since for Luhmann religion provides ultimate rationales for
the society as a whole, this independence of other functional spheres may appear, from the point of view of religion, as a negation of religion. The religious system's
relation to the other subsystems of modern society thus
becomes a problem for religion. This briefly is Luhmann's
formulation and approach to what is more commonly known as
the problem of "religion and society" or, more specifically,
the problem of "secularization."[42]

Luhmann analyzes the performance of religion, that is,
its relation to the other subsystems of society under the
term, *diakonia*. The term is broadly conceived to include
all those services that, under the umbrella of religion,
respond to problems engendered in other subsystems of society but not solved there.[43] He thinks of such services as
being provided primarily to individual people who are the
victims of such structural problems as opposed to the subsystems themselves. Such restriction to individual problems
ostensibly keeps the religious system from interfering too
much with the other subsystems. However, one may well ask
if Luhmann's concept of religious performance could not be
broadened just at this point to include instances like the
activities of certain sections of the Roman Catholic Church
in Latin America, activities that certainly go beyond
individual charity. The question has a politico-economic
counterpart: one may ask if religion need restrict itself
to a kind of religious "unemployment insurance" or whether
it can also proceed to certain forms of "state ownership" in
its quest to respond religiously to the problems engendered
in other subsystems.

Be that as it may, Luhmann does assert that any religious performance in modern society must be accepted and

processed by the subsystem towards which it is directed.
This conception flows out of his formulation of performance
as an exchange process.   If this condition is to be met,
then the religious performance must to some extent accommodate itself to the requirements of the subsystem in question. Such accommodation can lead to discrepancies with the
religious function.   Thus, for example, fighting for the
elimination of political and economic injustice on religious
grounds can lead to accusations and perceptions of the performance action as just a disguised form of political activity that uses religion as an excuse. In short, for Luhmann,
performance and function can interfere with each other.
     The picture is completed by a consideration of reli-
gious reflection. For Luhmann, theology fills this place.
As nas been pointed out, reflection becomes a problem in a
repidly changing, functionally differntiated society because the continuity necessary for identity is more difficult to formulate in such circumstances. Especially the
increasingly visible contingency of all identity becomes a
problem. Luhmann sees this as being particularly the case
in theological reflection. As might be expected, he believes that the principal difficulty lies in the interfer-
ence of adequate reflection with specifically the fulfillment of the function of religion. For Luhmann, adequate
response to the performance and reflection relations threatens the response to function because the former tend, in
some sense, to accommodate themselves to the exigencies of
modern society, exigencies that contradict the claim
expressed in the religious function, that religious
interpretation is applicable to the society as a whole. It
is in the light of this analysis that the problems raised in
the following work must be seen. Luhmann's "critique" of
religion in modern society is based on the changed and chang-

ing socio-structural conditions in which religion must function, perform, and reflect.

The ideas surrounding differentiation and its consequences are elaborations of Luhmann's systems theory. This
theory is however only one of three partial theories that
together make up the Luhmannian theory of society. The
other two partial theories are the theory of evolution and
the theory of communication.[44] The fact that there are
three theories is not fortuitous. The three theories
correspond to what Luhmann sees as the three dimensions of
the world. They are the objective, the temporal, and the
social dimension.[45] For Luhmann, they are not reducible to
one another. A negation in one of the dimensions does not
automatically imply a negation in either of the other two.
Luhmann uses this triad to replace other such alternative
fundamental   distinctions   as   experience/action   and
theory/practice. Accordingly, his theory of society has
three partial theories that are not reducible to one
another. The theory of systems approaches the objective
dimension of the world, the theory of evolution the temporal
dimension, the theory of communication the social dimension.

As has been mentioned, social systems in this theory
consist of communicative actions. These are founded on what
Luhmann, based on Parsons,[46] calls double contingency or
double selectivity. The idea expressed here is that the
action of a system (whether social or personal) is always a
selection from more than one possibility and that when two
systems exchange selections, they do so on the basis that
each has such a choice. Put in terms of people, this means
that a person in social interaction can choose whether or
not to accept what an interaction partner communicates to
him, can also choose what he communicates himself, and
assumes that the person with whom he is communicating also

has these choices.

For Luhmann, the communicative process assumes that the experience of the communicating partners is not the same. If it were, there would be no need or basis for communication. In the act of communicating, a contingent selection of one partner is offered to the other partner as a basis for the latter's own further selections. Language, for Luhmann, is not only a way of articulating the offered selection, but also provides a way of accepting or rejecting the selection. The partner addressed can indicate yes or no. Language allows that all information can be expressed positively or negatively. Luhmann calls mechanisms that can duplicate information in this way, codes.[47] The possibility of accepting or rejecting a communicative offering through the use of codes leads to a consideration of what motivates such acceptance or rejection. On what basis is the selection of one partner accepted as a basis of further selections by the other partner? This is Luhmann's way of inquiring into the conditions of *successful* communication.

Luhmann asserts that in primitive or simple societies successful communication was assured partly on the basis of language, partly on the basis of strict rules in interaction processes, and in any case on a restricted and shared view of reality that limited the number of possibilities for experience and action (i.e., selection). The introduction of writing brought a tremendous increase in the communicative possibilities, above all, because communication was thereby made possible beyond the immediate face-to-face interaction situation. This expansion of communicative possibilities, concomitant with the advent of stratified societies, resulted in the development of additional code mechanisms whose function was to make possible successful communication even in non-face-to-face communication. These

mechanisms Luhmann calls symbolically generalized *communications media*. These are ways of assuring the successful
transmission of selections using symbolic codes that are
applicable in a great many situations and for a great many
different communications.

Luhmann's favourite examples of these media are truth,
love, money, and political power. In each of these, selections are accepted because they are communicated through one
of these media: he sees it this way because it is true; he
does this because he loves her; she accepts what he does
with that object because he bought it and therefore owns it;
he does as the judge tells him because of the power vested
in him. Each communications medium is based on a code which
sets out the rules for the use of the medium. If one follows the rules of the code, the communication should be
successful. The codes in turn are based on binary schemata
that allow the acceptance or rejection of a communication on
the basis of the code. Examples of these are right/wrong
(in the politico-legal sense), true/false, love/not love,
own/not own. In each case the second term of the pair is
simply the negation of the first which is *valued positively*.

Luhmann's way of explaining the differentiation of
these codes is dependent on his analysis of experience and
action. For him, these are different modes of attribution
and not two different kinds of real process. What is attributed are selections. When a system attributes a selection
to its environment, the selection is experienced by the
system. When, on the other hand, the attribution is to the
system itself, the selection is the action of the system.
Luhmann considers that the media are differentiated on the
basis of whether they transmit experienced selection or
acted selection and whether these are accepted as the basis
for further experience or action. Thus for example, truth

brings about that the experience of one partner is accepted
as a basis for further experience of the other partner.
Love brings about that the experience of one partner is
accepted as a basis of the action of the other. Each type
of transmission can be the basis for more than one medium.
Luhmann therefore does not restrict the number of possible
communications media to four.

These communications media form one of the major bases
for the functional differentiation of modern society. All
functional spheres operate around a binary schema. Most of
them develop elaborated symbolic codes and corresponding
media which serve as a point of reference for their differentiation from the rest of society. The connection between
medium formation and functional differentiation becomes
important in Luhmann's treatment of religion in modern society. In the following work, Luhmann argues that difficulties in articulating the medium of religion, faith, have
certain consequences for the adjustment of the religious
system to modern society.[48]

To round out this introduction to Luhmann's theory of
society consideration must be given to his theory of social
evolution, especially since this theory plays a vital but
somewhat inarticulated background role in the following
work.[49] Evolution for Luhmann springs out of the difference
between system and environment. Specifically, it springs
from the fact that there are other systems in the environment of any given system and these systems experience and
act differently. We have seen that this incongruence is
also at the heart of all communication. It is seen as the
basis for evolution because a change in any one system (not
just social or personal!) implies that the environment of
all other systems is also changed, thereby creating the
conditions for further change in these other systems. Ulti-

mately, evolution is based on the excessive complexity of
the world and the corresponding contingency of all selections.

     This system/environment foundation of evolutionary
change has an important consequence for Luhmann's view of
the evolution of societies: each subsystem's change is a
response, in part, to changes in the inner-societal environment. Societal evolution is therefore something that must
be considered on the level of society as a whole and not
just at the level of one of its subsystems.   The evolution
of a subsystem, for instance of the religious system, cannot
be analyzed properly if it is considered in isolation from
the society of which the system is a part.

     Evolution, for Luhmann, is not a continuous, causal
process.   As such, it is not necessary or unilinear.   Drop-
ping the conception of a cause and effect chain also implies
a lack of irreversibility and of its characterization as a
movement from the simple to the complex.   Socio-cultural
evolution is here rather a mechanism for the change of societal structures.   It is a mechanism that uses chance to
induce structural changes in the sense that events which do
not occur with specific reference to a system can be used to
induce structural change in that system.   The reference to
chance indicates that Luhmann's theory of socio-cultural
evolution has certain similarities with theories of non-or-
ganic and organic evolution.   This can be seen most clearly
in his designation of the specific mechanisms of evolution
as variation, selection, and retention or stabilization.
What fulfills these functions in the organic realm are genetic mutation, natural selection, and the reproductive
isolation of populations.   However, this parallel does not
lead him to a kind of "survival-of-the-fittest" social
Darwinism since, in the case of socio-cultural evolution,

what fulfills the three functions is quite different.

Luhmann puts elements of his own theory in these conceptual slots. The variation mechanism for socio-cultural
evolution is for him linguistic communication. The salient
feature of language is that it allows a great number of
possibilities to be expressed and at the same time allows
each possibility to be affirmed or negated.[50] Linguistic
communication, however, can change and has changed. The
introduction of writing vastly increased the range of such
communication as well as the number of possibilities that
could be expressed. The introduction of mass communication
media, especially printing, took such expansion even further. For Luhmann, these changes mean that the conditions
under which the selection and stabilization mechanisms operate are changed and therefore evolution itself changes. He
sees an evolution of evolution. The conditions for
socio-structural change are different for each set of historical circumstances because the evolutionary mechanisms
themselves undergo structural change, that is, evolution.

Luhmann's socio-cultural selection mechanism can be
deduced from his variation mechanism. Since variation is
based on communication, selection must be based on successful communication. The selection mechanism will therefore
be identical with the structures that assure such success.
With the advent of writing and the correlative socio-structural changes, this mechanism becomes increasingly identified with the communications media.

Finally, the construction and differentiation of social
systems is seen as the socio-cultural mechanism for stabilization. It will be remembered that a system is virtually
defined as a relatively stable reduction of complexity.
Systems establish and maintain themselves by stabilizing a
complexity gradient vis-a-vis their environments through

their selectivity. Increase in complexity implies increased
selectivity and increased selectivity is reflected in
changes in the extent and type of differentiation. Luhmann
therefore sees the response to the increased complexity
brought about by changes in the mechanisms for variation and
selection, as just outlined, in changes in the form of
primary differentiation. The shift from primarily
segmentary to primarily stratified to primarily functional
differentiation increases the stabilization power of a
society to correspond to the intensified variation and
selection. Thus, for instance, the development of
communications media is seen as correlating with the
emergence of stratified societies; and functional subsystems
in functionally differentiated society crystallize around
communications media and their elaborated codes.

     The evolution of the evolutionary mechanisms also in-
volves the degree to which the three operate independently
of each other, that is, the degree to which variation does
not automatically imply selection and selection does not
automatically favour stabilization. This factor allows
Luhmann to develop further his characterization of three
fundamental societal types. Archaic societies are characterized by a primacy of segmentary differentiation, restriction
to oral communication in face-to-face interaction, and lack
of elaborated media. The last feature indicates that these
societies do not separate variation and selection mechanisms. Successful communication is assured through restrictive rules of interaction and a simple view of reality.
Linguistic communication operates as both variation and
selection mechanism. In what Luhmann calls advanced civilizations, the development of media makes the separation of
the two possible. Instead, the separation of selection and
stabilization mechanisms becomes a problem. The media are

embedded in a societal structure that differentiates primarily according to strata and not functional spheres. Communicative success is tied to conformity with this global
societal structure and the moral, religious, and cosmic
interpretations that support it. In both these instances,
Luhmann sees barriers to socio-structural change that become
much weaker in modern, functionally differentiated society.
Most of the major communications media are now aligned with
specific, relatively independent subsystems. This structure
allows for stabilization under a greater variety of conditions. A selection can be stabilized with reference to only
one functional sphere of society and compatibility requirements are now limited to those between functional subsystems, not specific selections. The three mechanisms can
operate with some independence, making very rapid change not
only possible but even probable.

Even though Luhmann's analysis of three types of society accords with a rough periodization, it cannot be con-
cluded that he therefore conceives evolution to be a process, let alone a continuous one. The view of evolution as
a mechanism or as a set of mechanisms is an attempt to get
away from this idea of evolution as a process. There are
several important consequences of this position, of which I
shall mention but a few. Perhaps most important in the
present context is that Luhmann's theory does not claim to
be able to predict the future course of social change: the
analysis of evolutionary mechanisms does not of itself permit conclusions as to what kinds of changes these mechanisms
will produce. A corollary of this conclusion is that the
theory cannot fully explain the development of one society
out of another, only certain key correlations that
accompanied the transition and the characteristics of the
transition itself. Thus, for example, the development of

the European portion of modern society out of medieval Western European society can be described and to some extent
explained, but not presented as a causal process with a more
or less inevitable outcome.[51]

A second consequence has to do with the position of
religion in modern society. Luhmann presents his analysis
of why religion is having certain difficulties in the new
context of this society, but he does not thereby presume
that he can prescribe a course of action. His way of putting this in the following work is that he can ask certain
questions of religion and of theologians, but that it is for
these to come up with the final answers. He does not, for
instance, insist that the religious system model itself on
the modern economic system in order to become more "up to
date." In fact, elsewhere he suggests that the religious
system may even be preserving certain options for society as
a whole, options such as an insistence on the idea of perfection as the ultimate goal of all social action as opposed to
the idea of open-ended development which otherwise domi-
nates, especially in the economic domains of modern society.[52]

This presentation of key elements of Luhmann's theory
of socio-cultural evolution concludes this overview of the
foundational concepts of Luhmann's general theory of society
and religion. Although part of what has been presented is
indeed very abstract and may seem little related to the
study of religion, it is hoped that this introduction will
help the reader to a better understanding of the theoretical
ground out of which Luhmann's approach to religion grows.
Such an understanding is especially important since Luhmann
locates religion as a societal phenomenon at a very
fundamental level of social structure. Part of the justification for the abstractness is just this necessity for ana-

lyzing the point where the religious motivation and the
societal function meet. Locating this point of intersection
at a more specified level, such as the integration of society or the satisfaction of a need for interpretation,[53]
would lead to the difficulties that such other functional
definitions have encountered, particularly the difficulty of
reducing religious phenomena to no more than a specified
socio-structural role, ignoring those aspects of religion
that address the very possibility of any structure whatsoever. By going beyond such partial functional definitions,
Luhmann hopes to account adequately for the social dimensions of religion in all societies while at the same time
leaving open, within the terms of his overall theory, a
domain which is still properly religious, which defies sociological or psychological reduction and allows religion both
a legitimizing and a critical role with respect to the social structures that are a condition for its possibility.

Peter Beyer
May, 1983

NOTES

[1] Five major articles have been published in English: "The Future Cannot Begin: Temporal Structures in Modern Society," *Social Research* 43 (1976), 130-152; "Generalized Media and the Problem of Contingency," in *Explorations in General Theory in Social Science: Essays in Honor of Talcott Parsons*, ed. Jan J. Loubser, Rainer C. Baum, Andrew Effrat, and Victor M. Lidz (New York: Free Press, 1976), II, 507-532; "Differentiation of Society," *Canadian Journal of Sociology* 2 (1977), 29-54; "A General Theory of Organized Systems", ed. Geert Hofstede and M. Sami Kassem (Assen-Amsterdam: Van Gorcum, 1976), pp. 96-113; and "Temporalization of Complexity," in *Sociocybernetica*, ed. R. Felix Geyer and Johannes van der Zouwen (Leiden: Nijhoff, 1978), pp. 95-111. One minor article on religious theory has been translated into English: "Institutionalized Religion in the Perspective of Functional Sociology," in *The Church as Institution*, ed. Gregory Baum and Andrew Greeley, *Concilium: Religion in the Seventies*, New Series, Vol. I, No. 10 (New York: Herder & Herder, 1974), 45-55, translated by Francis McDonagh. Several articles have been translated in a collection of articles: N. Luhmann, *The Differentiation of Society*, trans. Stephen Holmes and Charles Larmore (New York: Columbia Univ. Press, 1982). Finally two of Luhmann's shorter books have been translated in one volume: N. Luhmann, *Trust and Power*, ed. Tom Burnes, intro. Gianfranco Poggi, trans. Howard Davis, John Raffan, and Kathryn Rooney (New York - Toronto: Wiley, 1979).

[2] See Karl-Wilhelm Dahm, Niklas Luhmann, Dieter Stoodt, *Religion - System und Sozialisation* (Neuwied: Luchterhand, 1972), pp. 15-132; and Niklas Luhmann, *Funktion der Religion* (Frankfurt: Suhrkamp, 1977), pp. 77-181.

[3] For a discussion of this and the following under the heading of *supertheories*, see Luhmann, "Soziologie der Moral," in *Theorietechnik und Moral*, ed. Niklas Luhmann and Stephan H. Pfürtner (Frankfurt: Suhrkamp, 1978), pp. 9-27 (17).

[4] See Luhmann, "Systemtheorie, Evolutionstheorie und Kommunikationstheorie," in *Soziologische Auklärung: Aufsätze zur Theorie der Gesellschaft*, Vol. II (Opladen: Westdeutscher Verlag, 1975), pp. 193-203. See also below, p. xxx.

[5] See Talcott Parsons, *Societies: Evolutionary and Comparative Perspectives* (Englewood Cliffs, N.J.:

Prentice-Hall, 1966), pp. 5-29; and "On the Concept of
Value-Commitments," *Sociological Inquiry* XXXVIII (1968),
135-160.

[6]For the most comprehensive treatment to date, see
Luhmann, "Einführende Bemerkungen zu einer Theorie
symbolisch generalisierter Kommunikationsmedien," in
Soziologische Aufklärung II, pp. 170-192.

[7]See Luhmann, "Selbst-Thematisierungen des
Gesellschaftssystems," in *Ibid.*, pp. 72-102 (esp. pp. 74,
83f.).

[8]See Luhmann, "Frühneuzeitliche Anthropologie:
Theorietechnische Lösungen für ein Evolutionsproblem der
Gesellschaft," in *Gesellschaftsstruktur und Semantik:
Studien zur Wissenssoziologie der modernen Gesellschaft*
(Frankfurt: Suhrkamp, 1980), I, 162-234.

[9]For a critique in English, see Rudolf J. Siebert,
"Parsons' Analytical Theory of Religion as Ultimate
Reality," in *Sociology and Human Destiny: Essays on
Sociology, Religion, and Society*, ed. Gregory Baum (New
York: Seabury Press, 1980), pp. 27-55.

[10]Because of the extent of this kind of critique, it
cannot be explored here in detail. Perhaps the best known
of this large corpus is Jürgen Habermas' critique. See, for
instance, "Theorie der Gesellschaft oder Sozialtechnologie?
Eine Auseinandersetzung mit Niklas Luhmann," in Habermas and
Luhmann, *Theorie der Gesellschaft oder Sozialtechnologie -
Was leistet die Systemforschung?* (Frankfurt: Suhrkamp,
1971), pp. 142-284. As a further example, see Franz
Maciejewski, "Sinn, Reflexion und System: Über die
vergessene Dialektik bei Niklas Luhmann," *Zeitschrift für
Soziologie* I (1972), pp. 139-155. For a critique of
Luhmann's use of Parsonian theory, see Stefan Jensen,
"Interpenetration - Zum Verhältnis personaler und sozialer
Systeme?" *Zeitschrift für Soziologie* VII (1978),
pp. 116-129.

[11]What follows is taken from Luhmann, "Soziologie der
Moral," pp. 18-45. For details of who is included in the
"humanistic tradition" and further examples of this
comparison, see this study.

[12]See "Vorbereitende Bemerkungen zu einer Theorie der
kommunikativen Kompetenz," in Habermas and Luhmann, *Theorie
der Gesellschaft*, pp. 101-142.

[13]See as an example, Luhmann, "Gesellschaft," in *Soziologische Aufklärung: Aufsätze zur Theorie sozialer Systeme*, Vol. I, 4th ed. (Opladen: Westdeutscher Verlag, 1974), pp. 137-153.

[14]I say "is closer to being" because complexity in Luhmann's theory cannot be understood adequately merely on the basis of this comparison. See Luhmann, "Komplexität," in *Soziologische Aufklärung* II, pp. 204-220 (esp. 107f).

[15]See, for instance, Luhmann, "Funktionale Methode und Systemtheorie," in *Soziologische Aufklärung* I, 31-53; "Selbst-Thematisierungen des Gesellschaftssystems," and "Komplexität," in *Soziologische Aufklärung* II, pp. 72-102, 204-220; and "Sinn als Grundbegriff der Soziologie," in Habermas, Luhmann, *Theorie der Gesellschaft*, pp. 25-100.

[16]See above, note 2.

[17]See Luhmann, "Moderne Systemtheorien als Form gesamtgesellschaftlicher Analyse," in *ibid.*, pp. 7-24 (10f).

[18]Cf. W. Ross Ashby, *An Introduction to Cybernetics* (London: Methuen, 1964), esp. pp. 202-218.

[19]See Luhmann, "Sinn als Grundbegriff der Soziologie," in Habermas, Luhmann, *Theorie der Gesellschaft*.

[20]Cf. Luhmann, "Das Phänomen des Gewissens und die normative Selbstbestimmung der Persönlichkeit," in Dorothee Sölle, et. al., *Religionsgespräche: Zur gesellschaftlichen Rolle der Religion* (Neuwied: Luchterhand, 1975), pp. 95-119.

[21]See Luhmann, *Funktion der Religion*, p. 21.

[22]Thus in the work translated here, p. 4.

[23]*Funktion der Religion*, p. 21.

[24]For the following discussion, see Luhmann, "Komplexität," in *Soziologische Aufklärung* II, pp. 204-220.

[25]See Luhmann, "Soziologie als Theorie sozialer Systeme," in *Soziologische Aufklärung* I, pp. 113-136 (esp. 116f.). The German term "erfassen" has the normal meaning of grasping or seizing. It has been translated here as "realize" in order to emphasize the creative character, in Luhmann's theory, of this "Erfassen."

[26]For Luhmann's use of the Husserlian concept of "appresentation," see *Funktion der Religion*, pp. 22ff.

[27]See below, pp. 93ff.

[28]See *Funktion der Religion*, p. 41f; and "Soziologie der Moral," in *Theorietechnik und Moral*, p. 81ff.

[29]See Talcott Parsons, *The Structure of Social Action*, 2 vols. (New York: Free Press, 1968).

[30]Compare in the following work, pp. 8 and 54.

[31]See, for instance, *Funktion der Religion*, p. 16f.

[32]See Luhmann, "Funktionale Methode und Systemtheorie," in *Soziologische Aufklärung* I, pp. 31-53, for Luhmann's ideas of function and functional method.

[33]See Luhmann, "Reflexive Mechanismen," in *ibid.*, pp. 92-112.

[34]For a discussion of this and the following, see *Funktion der Religion*, pp. 27ff.

[35]For Luhmann's analysis of the origins of this development, see Luhmann, *Gesellschaftsstruktur und Semantik*, Vol. I, 166, 176ff.

[36]A good discussion can be found in Luhmann, "Differentiation of Society," *Canadian Journal of Sociology* II (1977), 29-54.

[37]See the discussion of communications media, below, pp. xxxivff.

[38]See Luhmann's analysis under the Parsonian heading of "inclusion" in *Funktion der Religion*, pp. 232ff.

[39]See below, p. 31.

[40]For a thorough analysis of these relations as they appear in the religious system, see *Funktion der Religion*, pp. 54-66. A general consideration of these relations can be found in "Differentiation of Society," pp. 35-38.

[41]See *Funktion der Religion*, p. 33f.

[42]For a comprehensive study, see *ibid.*, pp. 225-271.

[43]See *ibid.*, pp. 57-59.

[44]See Luhmann, "Systemtheorie, Evolutionstheorie, Kommunikationstheorie," in *Soziologische Aufklärung* II, pp. 193-203.

[45]For an indication of the derivation of these dimensions, see the discussion of their relation to the concept of meaning in "Sinn als Grundbegriff der Soziologie" in Habermas, Luhmann, *Theorie der Gesellschaft*, pp. 48ff.

[46]See, for example, Talcott Parsons, *The Social System*. (New York: Free Press, 1951), p. 10f.

[47]For this and much of the following discussion, see Luhmann, "Einführende Bemerkungen zu einer Theorie symbolisch generalisierter Kommunikationsmedien," in *Soziologische Aufklärung* II, pp. 170-192 (172f).

[48]See below, pp. 54-63.

[49]The most illuminating contributions in this regard are Luhmann, "Geschichte als Prozeß und die Theorie sozio-kultureller Evolution," in *Historische Prozesse*, ed. Karl-Georg Faber and Christian Meier (Munich: Deutscher Taschenbuch Verlag, 1978), pp. 413-440; and "Evolution als Geschichte," in *Soziologische Aufklärung* II, pp. 150-169. The present discussion is based on these.

[50]See the discussion of communication, above, pp. xxxivff.

[51]Cf. Luhmann, *Gesellschaftsstruktur und Semantik*, pp. 9-234.

[52]See *Funktion der Religion*, p. 207f.

[53]For Luhmann's critique, see *Ibid.*, pp. 9ff.

For some time now, religious studies has taken for granted that human action in general is influenced by social conditions. This applies as well to human religious action. This conditionality is dealt with by some in the concept of the church and is hereby restricted to the "external" aspects of human existence. By contrast, the actual locus of religious experience is assumed to be internal and therefore free from the influence of societal determinations. Accordingly, "faith" becomes an "internal" affair of the person, whether or not his action is ecclesiastically organized. In this way, religion and church are differentiated on the basis of experience and action. Interrelationships between experience and action are of course not excluded. On the contrary, they are quite definitely presupposed.

As regards its origins, this conception can be understood as a correlative of the differentiation between religion and politics in society. Not only was religion a matter for the church as opposed to the state, but it was supposedly even further beyond the scope of society and politics because it was the "internal affair" of the person. Protestant doctrine especially stabilized this separation in its concepts of faith and church. It was hereby in tune with the increasing functional differentiation of the societal system. This latter development has resulted in what we today call "bourgeois society," "industrial society" or "technicoscientific civilization."

However, this distinction between internal and external is a defensive conceptualization. As such, it must be analyzed with more abstract sociological categories. Neither

the empirical conclusions nor the theoretical conceptions of
modern social research allow such a simple separation of
"internal" and "external" or of "experience" and "action."
This is not because social research has abandoned these
concepts as useless, but rather because it *works with them*.
These examples of internal/external and experience/action
therefore show that the possible relationships between sociological theory and religious dogmatics are closer, more
abstract, more fruitful, and more dangerous than is commonly
assumed.

The *difference between internal and external* is central
to every kind of systems theory. It is discussed on both
the conceptual and empirical levels. It is applied to
whatever system is under discussion and is controlled analytically. The conceptual consequences are worked out in the
form of structure and process analyses, input/output models,
theories of information processing, selectivity, complexity
differences, and so forth. Further elaboration of these
things is not necessary here.

Moreover, the distinction between experience and action
can also no longer serve as a self-evident and ultimate
point of departure. However, the social sciences have completely abandoned this distinction to the extent that they
have been dominated by behaviourism. As a result, the scientific situation is less clear in this case. In fact, this
situation seems to support the idea that sociology is a
science limited to the study of action. As such, it would
be capable of examining the active aspect of religion in the
social context, but could not approach "actual religious
experience." This conclusion would however be basing itself
on a view of social-scientific theory that has since been
surpassed and was never entirely applicable in the first
place.

Let us for the moment remain with the distinction
between experience and action. Especially in more recent
psychology and social psychology, theoretical models are
becoming more and more common, in which the interdependence
of cognitive and motivational processes is of central importance[1]. This interdependence means that experience and
action can no longer be distinguished as different kinds of
real processes (for instance, internal and external ones)[2].
Instead, the distinction presupposes processes of attribution that first determine what is going to be experienced as
experience and what is going to be treated as action. In
this case, we can again use concepts derived from psychological research, namely the distinction between internal
and external attribution[3]. However, in this state of
abstraction, these concepts are not yet suited for our purpose. An appropriate extension of these concepts would see
action as a process of selection, the selectivity of which
is attributed to the system. Experience would be a process
of selection, the selectivity of which is attributed to the
environment of the system[4]. Obviously, the attribution
cannot be done arbitrarily. It is nevertheless contingent
in the sense that there are various ways of doing it and in
the sense that it depends on cultural and social processes[5].

Some recent sociological theory has begun to incorporate such abstract concepts from systems theory. To the
extent that is has, the level of the discussion with religion and its dogmatic disciplines will shift. Sociology
will then be concerned with more than the "sociology of
religion" in the traditional sense. That is, it will no
longer restrict itself to such things as the roles, careers,
and communication problems of priests, or the pattern of
church organization and participation. Moreover, it will do
more than point out how symbols and institutions are ideo-

logical.   Rather, sociology can combine elements from the
sociology of action and the sociology of knowledge into a
new unity.   Sociological theory can thereby attain a level
of abstraction that will extend its horizon of interpretation.   It can analyze the assertions of religious dogmatics directly.

                                   II

    Neither the distinction between "internal" and "exter-
nal" nor the distinction between "experience" and "action"
can be used to ground a being outside of society.   We are
therefore dependent on the concept of society.   We must
begin with its analysis.
    Society is that social system that ultimately regulates
all the relations of the human being to the world.   Society
is the social condition for the constitution of meaningful
being-in-the-world.   To the extent that one uses the concepts of systems theory to conceive this constitution, one
also conceives society[6].   The concept of system brings the
difference between within and without, between environment
and system into the analysis of constitution.   One can think
of this difference as a complexity gradient in which the
environment is always more complex than the system itself.
The difference between possibility and reality is one of the
ways in which the system makes this complexity gradient
meaningful for itself.   In other words, a *modal generalization of reality* is basic to the meaningful processing of
experience.   According to this generalization, everything
given emerges only with reference to other possibilities.
Meaning is only constituted when the (implicit) reference to
other possibilities is constituted as well.   This constant
openness to other possibilities is one of the "costs" of a
relation between system and environment that is consciously

selective. Moreover, this openness varies with the kind of selection made.

The model generalization of reality constitutes the world as a whole; that is it refers to the system and its environment together. The difference between reality and possibility therefore in no way coincides with the difference between system and environment. Rather, the difference between reality and possibility is used to organize system and environment. Within the realm of the possible, what is at any time possible depends on the implied "conditions of possibility." These, on the one hand, cannot be set arbitrarily since they are dependent on structures. On the other hand, they can be stated in many different ways. There can be logical, cognitive, legal, economic, or political conditions of possibility. The conditions of possibility can be the will of another, one's own will, God's will, or whatever. They are generalized insofar as they are compatible with very diverse states of affairs. For even if the world changes, the possible can to a certain extent still remain possible. Modal generalization can represent the above-mentioned complexity gradient in that it makes it possible to constitute meaning with reference to several conditions of possibilitiy at the same time, and to vary these conditions as required. Through variation of such conditions of possibility, what is possible within the system can be distinguished from what is possible in the environment. In addition, the difference between what is possible in the system and what is possible in the environment can change in the course of evolution.

From what has just been said, it is apparent that a precise analysis already becomes quite complicated in its beginnings. The analysis involves concepts from systems theory, concepts arising out of the analysis of meaning,

concepts from modality theory, and concepts from theories of
evolution. However, there does not seem to be any other way
of getting a sufficiently powerful conceptual basis for the
analysis of society and religion. We have here only presented a brief outline of the beginnings of such a conceptual basis. With the help of these beginnings, it is possible to conceive the relation of world, system, and environment as a relation that uses structures and processes to
select from more than one possibility; and it is further
possible to conceive this selectivity itself as again variable. Herewith, the concept of society can become more
precise. Society is that social system which grounds its
own selectivity in that it constitutes meaning and thereby
synchronizes the generalization of possibilities with social
structures and processes.

                                    III

    In all pre-modern societies familiar to us, the func-
tion of religion is ultimately connected with this combination of constitution and reduction of a selective relation.
This combination is central to any society. The world is
experienced religiously. Social action, if it is not religiously justified, is nevertheless restricted in its selectivity by religious ideas. From the empirical evidence, it
would not be correct to assume complete coincidence of religion and meaningful action[7] or of religion and society.
However, in these societies, religious commitments fulfill
the function of the societal system. Other kinds of experience and action in the polity, the economy, and the family
are able to find their own domain within these societies on
the basis of these religious commitments[8].

    Thus far not much has been said. Such a formal under-
standing does not allow the deduction of contents or descrip-

tions, nor does it allow the explanation or prediction of
religious facts. It does not tell us what religion "is"[9].
This is neither an accident nor is it the fault of the
theory. On the contrary, it has been one of the conditions
of societal evolution that the various answers arrived at by
diverse territorial societies have not only been possible
but have also functioned with more or less good prospects
for evolution. The difficulty with the theory is therefore
to be found in the matter itself. The immense range and
variation of religious ideas is an aspect of the societal
character of religion - at least it was.

The function of religion refers to a specific problem
that society must solve. In the light of this problem of
reference, we can arrive at further formal characterizations
and even historical specifications of religion in spite of
the many functionally equivalent possibilities for religion.
For this purpose we can work with the distinction between
indeterminate and determinate complexity and the distinction
between latent and manifest function.

A system/environment relation in which complexity is
both constituted and reduced must ultimately be indeterminate because the structures of the world are dependent on
the structures of the system and vice versa. Since all
modalizations and selective determinations are dependent on
it, the societal system cannot be based on a determinate
environment. Therefore, the ultimate functional level of
social systems must be one at which indeterminate complexity
is transformed into determinate or at least determinable
complexity[10]. This does not mean that already existing
"underlying structures of reality" are merely "thematized"[11]. Instead, discreteness, typology, discontinuity,
boundary, and therefore "otherness" are actually produced in
the first place[12]. Religious qualities gravitate towards

this transformation function[13].   Cultural structures with
precisely this functional reference are religions.   The
function of religion refers to the determinability of the
world[14].

Because of this function of reformulating indeterminate
complexity, religion remains bound to the level of the societal system as a whole.   Religion has not changed in this
connection, but rather because of this connection.   It is
precisely this reference to the system as a whole that
explains the evolutionary changes and historical fortunes of
religion.   The   following   analyses   are   based   on   this
assumption[15].   In   the   course   of   the   evolution   towards
greater complexity, the place-value of society as a whole
among the social systems changes.   Above all, as internal
differentiation and differentiation of levels increase, the
need decreases for the kind of selective determinations that
must, or at least can, be produced for the entire society at
this highest level of system construction.   The need as well
as the possibility for such uniform formulations decreases
with increasing complexity of the societal system.   For
religion, two possibilities result from this situation: it
will be generalized with the totality of the societal system
and/or it will be called upon only in certain situations.
The *whole* only becomes significant *occasionally*; it is a
part in itself.   This calls for a shift in one's thinking, a
shift from representation to reflection.

This functional way of conceiving religion goes beyond
the familiar controversy as to whether religion relieves
anxiety and uncertainty or whether it generates them to
begin with[16].   Both are in a certain sense correct.   Religion reformulates the conditions for insecurity.   It interprets events and possibilities in a way that correlates them
with the meaningful orientation of people.   It thereby makes

an increase in acceptable insecurity possible. The need for
this accomplishment is connected and varies with two
factors. First there is the stage of development of the
society. This development entails increasing complexity and
contingency of other possibilities. Second, there are the
structures of religion itself.

In very early stages of the development of human society, the transformation of the indeterminate, as it were,
bypasses contingency. The problem of contingency is avoided
with a belief about reality that is more or less lacking in
alternatives. Religious experience is accordingly geared
towards disappointment, surprise, and anxiety. The problem
then becomes one of maintaining the social interaction patterns in spite of anxiety and disappointed expectations.
The function of religion is not yet, as it is later, performed with the help of rather bold interpretations. It is
achieved by *immediate sacralization of the problem*.
Examples of this are the tabooing of weak points in social
order, of transitions, of hybridizations, of the unclas-
sifiable, of anomalies[17]. The rituals provided for this
purpose carry religion. Those simple societies which exhibit few rituals[18] are also those with limited religiosity.
Rituals are processes of important ceremonial communication
that control or depict as controlled the risk of all communication: the possible misuse of the symbols[19]. Where they
use language, they do so in a "de-linguisticized" form.
They cancel the achievement of language when it becomes
risky and they do this without giving the achievement up.
They thereby form the basic structure of condensed sociality. Because of this, they also recede in looser forms of
social life[20]. Moreover, rituals put the communication
necessary for their performance under the sanction of what
is external and terrible, the appearance of which would

constitute   a   breach   of   the   ritual.   Thereby   the   double
contingency   of   all   sociality   is   eliminated   or   at   least
minimized.   The   risk   of   the   linguistic   use   of   signs   is
neutralized   until   effective   ways   of   selecting   are   developed
even   for   relatively   improbable   situations.   These   selectors
have   historically   taken   the   form   of   symbolically   generalized
communications   media[21].   A   late   variant   of   the   ritualistic
form   is   the   mythical   recitative.   This   is   a   standardized,
rhythmic,   and   rhapsodic   oral   tradition   as   for   instance   in
the   Homeric   epics.   Here   a   mythical   recitative   provided   a
point   of   contrast   for   the   philosophers   who   were   striving   for
an   object   oriented   communication[22].

As   a   society   becomes   more   complex,   its   generalizations
also   increase.   More   possibilities   become   visible.   One
becomes   conscious   of   reality   as   to   an   increasing   extent
contingent,   as   "also   possible   otherwise."   In   order   to   control   access   to   these   other   possibilities,   society   now
requires   devices   which   we   shall   call   *contingency   formulae*.
One   of   the   most   important   contingency   formulae   is   a   principle   of   political   legitimacy,   that   is,   a   formula   for   the
common   good.   Another   is   the   economic   principle   of   a   limited
supply   of   goods   (and   in   this   concrete   sense,   scarcity)[23].
Two   further   examples   are   the   normative   structures   of   law[24],
and   the   principle   of   limitationality   in   sci ce.   This
latter   is   a   presupposition   for   the   binary   yes/no   schema   of
logic[25].   Very   shortly   after   its   constitution,   this   schema
was   applied   to   the   problem   of   possibility   itself[26].   Then,
in   the   form   of   the   possibile/impossibile   and   the
necessarium/contingens   dichotomies,   it   abstracted   the   theological   discussion   of   the   middle   ages   in   a   way   that   could   no
longer   be   controlled   by   religious   means.

Since   all   these   principles   have   until   now   been   stated
in   relatively   concrete   and   morally   imbued   terms,   the   problem

of contingency has not become fully transparent. Such
contingency formulae operate by reconstructing any amount of
complexity and contingency. This reconstruction takes the
form of reductions that determine complexity sufficiently to
make selections possible. For example, it is only when
someone can act contrary to expectations and when this can
be anticipated, that one gets the problems associated with
the setting of legal norms and with the handling of conflicts and violations through legal procedure. It is only
when one thing is done at the expense of another that the
problems of distribution, help, and gratefulness arise. It
is only when a yes excludes a no and vice versa that dialogue and argumentation result, producing a progression of
knowledge. Moreover, the institution of these contingency
formulae has been a matter for religion because it demands a
transformation of indeterminate into determinate complexity.
Nevertheless, within the spheres controlled by these formulae, an immediate religious orientation is superfluous and
even hindering to the extent that these spheres become structured. The peculiar relation between religion and these
formulae has held up until modern times. Founded on religion, they take over its function and at the same time disso-
ciate themselves from it. We may surmise that such a
conspicuous state of affairs will not go unnoticed in religious dogmatics. It must find expression in one form or
another, perhaps in the form of a negative judgment on the
"world."

A concept of religion that assigns *only one* functional
determination to religion is often criticized because of its
indeterminacy[27]. On the one hand, such a concept includes
too many ways of experiencing and acting that are usually
regarded as non-religious. On the other hand, a single,
abstract, functional specification says too little because

it does not grasp the internal variety of religion or the
limits of that variation. This weakness of functional
conceptualization cannot be alleviated by specifying "how"
the function is fulfilled: that is, for instance, by label-
ling religion as belief in superhuman entities. Such a
narrowing down of the function would only result in an
historically relative and no longer universally applicable
concept of religion. Instead, we would like to try to
correct and complexify the abstract onesidedness of a single
function by means of systems-theoretical analyses[28]. We
would like to incorporate into the theory of religion the
idea that every social system, including society, has more
than one problem to solve and must therefore fulfill more
than one function. The viability of a functional theory of
systems and religion will show itself in the extent to which
the analysis can go beyond the mere cataloguing of functions
and dysfunctions[29].

                              IV
One supplementary problem results from the structured
and limited capacity of all systems that experience meaning
and process information. The basic problem for such systems
lies in the complete indeterminacy of other possibilities.
These must be determined at least in certain respects in
order that selective processes of experience and action can
operate at all. This structural necessity cannot be avoided
by thematizing the function of such contingent determinations as a function within the system itself. For, in the
light of such a function, every determination would be interchangeable with others; that is, nothing could be decided.

We shall leave open the question of whether or not
there can be forms of reflection that confront this situation. All religions that we know have "ciphered" this problem, have hidden it and not used it as a basis for their own
variation. By ciphering we do not mean simply the use of

symbols as signs for something else, something not directly accessible to which they refer. Rather we mean the production of knowledge by means of reductive determination[30]. Ciphers mask and replace their origin. They are therefore not interchangeable with what they mean in the sense that signs are interchangeable with the signified. Thus religion cannot give "money" a try if "God" doesn't seem to be working any more. Formulated sociologically, the function of religion in the transformation of indeterminate into determinate or determinable complexity remains *latent* for religious experience as well as for religious dogmatics. The function is not itself thematized, but is rather "occupied" by religious themes. To formulate it yet another way: religious symbolism is not identical with what it symbolizes--with society itself (Durkheim) or with specifically religious functions within society[31]. It is not, for instance, an abridged form of sociological knowledge. This is understandable if one considers that thematizing the function would mean exposing religion itself to a comparison with other possibilities and thus to a substitution. Religion is therefore unaware of its function on the level of the sociological analysis which we take as our base here. In place of such awareness, we see the development of modes of understanding and interpretation which, under conditions yet to be discussed, coalesce into what we shall call the dogmatics of a religiously conceived world. Accordingly, religion does not develop through functional substitution, but rather through thematic generalization and abstraction.

Religious themes *require exegesis* as soon as they begin to function *independently of the situation*, that is, as soon as they aquire a significance beyond the regulation of immediate interaction among those present[32]. Recurrent use establishes conceptually similar patterns, spatially and

linguistically fixed points of orientation, and God-con-
cepts, all of which can be referred to again and again.
Their use must therefore be regulated. Correspondingly, the
contents of experience must be interpreted through such
themes. In older societies, this happens primarily in close
connection with rituals. Apart from these, it happens occasionally, through story-telling, in a fairly inconsistent
and unconscious way[33]. One cannot really speak of "faith"
in such cases[34]. It is only when experience is organized
much more independently of its context that a problem of
commitment (religio) actually arises. And along with this
problem, the problem of the professional supervision and
administration of these commitments also emerges. Further,
it is only when symbols, myths, and contingency formulae
become free of their contexts that a questioning of these
conceptions must be answered. Also, when the idea of perfection is applied to such conceptions, the contrast between
the perfect idea and concrete experience makes an evaluating
comparison possible[35]. Is this just? Is this a good king?
Is this how a friend acts? Does this happen according to
the will of God? A justifiable answer to such questions can
be expected.

For us, religious dogmatics is the verbal and conceptual apparatus that fulfills this interpretative function.
It is therefore not just one theological discipline among
others[36], and especially not an express contrast to moral
theology. Dogmatics are constructions that succeed rituals
on a higher level. They therefore make a certain de-ritualization of religion possible[37]. Along with rituals, they
control the risks of negation implied in all meaning, and
they are generalized through the use of language. Whereas
rituals *exclude negation* immediately through "de-linguis-
ticizing," the use of rhythm, bodily participation and

stereotypes, dogmatics *prohibit negation*. These prohibi-
tions are justified wherever possible; but where they are
not, they are at least secured in the dogmatic corpus in
terms of consistency and coherency. As a result, the social
control of explicit negation can become more important than
ensuring the relevance of faith[38]. The passage from rituals
to dogmatics consists in the "adaptive upgrading" (Parsons)
of the negation of negations. The selective pressure of
evolution on dogmatics as it were tests the stability of the
things which the particular dogmatic system holds to be
non-negatable. It tests this stability under increasing
demands for the specification of generalized problems, for
systematization, and for flexibility.

A dogmatics interprets in order to give an answer. It
works with functionally unanalyzed abstractions and is in
this respect unreflected. It does not thematize its societal function, but rather understands itself and its concept
of dogmatics only dogmatically. Thus, for instance, it
defines its concept of dogma in terms of revelation and the
teaching tradition of the church[39]. Furthermore, a dogmatics applies its material independently of context. That is,
it separates itself from the commitments which it interprets. The ways in which it can improve its performance
vary in the course of societal evolution. However, in the
light of the characteristics just described, it cannot do
this through reflection of its own contingency. It can
improve its performance through *greater degrees of freedom
in the handling of experiences and texts*. Religious dogmatics deals with themes, theses, and symbols. It is only
these, its objects, that refer to the world of experience.
In its advanced forms, it can use the articles of faith
which are already applicable free of context (e.g., the
Saviour is born) as the foundation for its own further move-

ment of thought. By systematizing and applying them, it can
give answers to newly arisen questions.

This peculiar function and structure of dogmatics,
which can also be observed in the field of law[40], cannot be
understood using the conventional scientific criticism of
dogmatics[41]. It is wrong to use science as the basis for
comparison.[42] Neither the contingency formula nor the communications medium of dogmatics allows one to conclude that
they are structures specializing in research. On the contrary, religious dogmatics interpret experiences and actions
that have to do with the indeterminate. They raise this
interpretation to a level of generalization which satisfies
the social demands for structural compatibility. We shall
return to the ways in which religious dogmatics might be
able to meet these demands, guided by examples. First,
however, some rather more sociological considerations are
still essential. These concern some aspects of the theory
of evolution (V), the "de-socialization" of the world with
the help of religious generalizations (VI), the external
differentiation of a societal subsystem with special
reference to religion (VII), and main directions for the
further specification of the problem peculiar to the
religious function (VIII).

                                    V

We shall begin with more or less classical theses of
sociology. The determinable *complexity* of a society and the
world possible for it increases in the course of evolution.
The problems which follow from such a development can only
be solved by an increasing differentiation of the societal
system. This statement accords with the insights of general
systems theory. The increase in *differentiation* is accomplished with the help of a change in the principle of

differentiation, a change which comes with the advent of
advanced cultures. This change consists in a gradual shift
from segmentary to stratifying, and finally to functional
creation of subsystems[43]. The differentiation of functionally specific subsystems is a prerequisite for surpassing a
very low threshold of societal evolution. This is the case
in the sphere of religion as elsewhere. As a correlative of
this development, the orientation of experience and action
is affected by a certain generalization on the symbolic-mo-
tivational level. Ideas that overlap the individual functional spheres must be generalized. Examples of such ideas
are house and town, sea-voyage and war, craft and cult.
Such ideas must also be conceived so that the single person
can be comprehended as an individual, an individual who is
relatively distinct from the social subsystems. Hereby the
cultural symbols and the orientation schema of a society
lose the immediacy and concreteness which they would have if
they remained tied to particular situations. Mechanisms for
the *respecification* of generalized orientation patterns must
be created, whose "application" sometimes becomes problematical. These can be found in the field of law, in a rising
educational system, and not least in the sphere of religion
which must now be more than ritual and cult. In this
system-structural context, religion reaches its definitive
form through the function of *interpretation*. It thereby
develops a functional equivalent for what above (p. 9) we
called immediate sacralization of the problem. Sacred
forms, if retained, are reformulated ethically, allegor-
ically, or symbolically.

Up to this point, we have been able to rely on an often
formulated sociological theory[44]. I would like to augment
it with two further proposals concerning *contingency formulae* and *communications media*. These concepts refer to

changes in the way that system and world are constituted in
relation to one another. The evolutionary conditions that
give rise to the growth of determinable complexity also
change the conditions under which indeterminate complexity
must   be   transformed   into   determinate   or   determinable
complexity. The contingency formulae responsible for this
transformation must allow for more possibilities in system
and world. These formulae must be abstracted from prevailing ideas about the nature of reality. However, the resulting norm concepts, disposition concepts, and possibility
concepts must not be so abstract as to lose their operative
function. This is a case of generalization and respecification in the sphere of modality.

Formulae that express dependencies and interdependencies also serve to transform indeterminable into determinable complexity. The many chaotic and arbitrary possibilities for being different are thereby reduced to determinable
relations. For example, scarcity makes the possibility of
having more or something different dependent on cost. This
dependency reduces the number of possibilities and also
makes interdependencies within systems calculable. A limita-
tional, binary logic reduces unrestricted possibilities for
forming true sentences to deducible forms. A principle of
political legitimacy reduces disorderly exercise of power to
responsible and authentic decision-making. The contingency
formulae for religion is the God-concept. Although this is
a similar reduction mechanism, it is not restricted to a
specific sphere but is rather world-universal. In the Western tradition, it has been formulated mainly in terms of a
correspondence between divine perfection and the variety and
perfection of the world[45]. However, by comparison with
other contingency formulae, this formulation alone does very
little towards setting up the kind of interdependencies that

can be systematically controlled.

More abstract contingency formulae also allow the recognition of experience and action as processes of *selection*
from more than one possibility. This selection changes the
possible into the actual. A good example of this can be
found in the shift in Greek legal thinking from thesmos to
nomos. This shift was associated with an increase in the
selectivity of the political institutions and decision-making processes[46]. Such changes imply that the communication
of selections has also become problematical. To the degree
that a person *chooses* what he experiences and does, and the
other person becomes aware of this, it is no longer obvious
that others will choose the same way or choose something
suitable. The connection between one person's choice and
another person's choice must now be guaranteed by special
mechanisms which we shall call *communications media*. In
Western tradition the chief examples of such communications
media are truth, love, money, art, and power[47]. Communications media are symbolic codes that set the rules for the
way in which symbols can be combined. Hereby they also
assure the "transmission" of selections. That is, they
bring about a situation in which ego adopts a selection by
alter as the premise for his own behaviour. A combination
of linguistic and motivational factors makes such an achievement possible. And the relations between these factors vary
with the evolutionary changes of the societal system.

In this connection, the previously outlined attribution
problems that lead to the differentiation of experience and
action become relevant. For if behaviour is recognized as
selection, it makes a difference whether this selection is
recorded as experience or action. That is, it makes a difference whether it is attributed to the world from which
behaviour merely "takes its bearings" or whether it is seen

as an output of the system, for example, as the "will" of
the actor.   In each case, the problem of appropriate
response-selection poses itself differently.   Accordingly,
each case requires a different communications medium.

The symbolic codes of the most important communications
media must therefore take account of this differentiation.
The type of specialization found in each medium depends on
this factor. For example, truth serves to transmit experience-selections as experience-selections in the sense that
an experience of alter is accepted by ego as a basis for his
own further experience. Power serves to convey action selections in the sense that alter, by means of an action-se-
lection attributed to her, can chose an action for ego.   If
this differentiation is recognized, truth can no longer be
promoted with force. Rather truth can now only be augmented
and verified by the rules and conditions established through
a code specialized for this medium[48]. And power can no
longer be justified on the basis of truth. Love, art, and
money are combination forms with clear rules of attribution.
In these cases, either the experience of alter must be
adopted in the action of ego (love), or vice versa (art,
money).

For a theory of religious dogmatics, the *doubling* of
the levels of symbol construction is of special importance.
We have already encountered this above on page 14f. with
regard to the function of dogmatics. Media-codes are symbolically generalized rules which set out what combinations of
symbols are permissible.   In the case of religion, these
symbols symbolize, for example, practical experiences of
faith (Glaubenserfahrungen). The level of the meaning-cre-
ating function of symbols is raised. This raising facili-
tates the creation of structure because it limits the possible.   At the same time it allows greater freedom in the

interpretation of what is immediately given and allows the functional differentiation of special spheres of communication.

Such differentiated and independent communications media contrast with everyday interaction which is normally not oriented to specific media. Rather these communications media only become relevant in certain kinds of situations. The connection between limitationality and truth is obvious, as is the connection between scarcity and money[49], and between legitimacy and power. It is also worth noting that, in the code of love, an "accidental" encounter appears as medium-specific contingency and is considered to be good. Further, art is dependent on natural or self-produced forms which allow a distinction of what is suitable or unsuitable[50].

All these concepts and analyses can only be mentioned here, not elaborated. We are concerned with what these briefly discussed lines of development may mean for religion and religious dogmatics. First we shall examine pre-modern advanced civilizations, specifically those which developed prototypes for highly developed religiosity[51].

VI

Before we detail the internal structure of the societal system, we must clarify the differentiation of this system out of the socially constituted world. It is likely that determinate meaning was originally constituted in very close and concrete connection with communication in social interaction. The certitude of meaning is not yet "individualized." Rather, the guarantees for such certitutde are immediately dependent on social resonance. In older societal systems, social relations are therefore projected more or less into the entire world. The basic dichotomies such as good and bad, near and far, friend and foe, familiar and unfamiliar, dichotomies which formulate the totality of the

world, are of a social nature. Even fundamental negations
are expressed as negated sociality. Beside this social
dimension, there is no *independent* temporal dimension (e.g.,
history) or objective dimension (e.g., causality)[52]. Social
constitution is both social *experience* and *thematization* of
the world. This constitution manifests itself in two ways
which can be analytically but not practically separated.
First, social partners are not restricted to interpersonal
relationships. Beside these, a profusion of "partners" is
experienced to whom one imputes the capacity for social
relationships, expectations, and intentional behaviour.
Familiar examples are totem animals, yam roots, and spirits
of the dead. The boundaries of the social world are not yet
identical with those of the human system[53]. Then, and this
projection was far more difficult to discard, social models
of order are imputed to the world as a whole. Examples are
the parent/child relationship or a standard for reward and
punishment. Together, the two ways of projection establish
a primacy of the social dimension in the meaningful determination of experience. Such a primacy precludes a socially
indifferent conception of the objective world, and above all
precludes the development of a more complex awareness of
time.

From the perspective of this analysis, the gradual
"de-socialization" of the world[54] is the result of complicated evolutionary processes. The congruence of the social
with the human no longer recognizes anything social outside
society (or societies). It is apparently a type of human
existence in the world that assumes many conditions. Historically it is in no way the rule but rather the exception.
In terms of symbolism, the de-socialization of the world is
to a large extent identical with the development of abstract
religious symbolism. Such symbolism is no longer uncondi-

tionally dependent upon direct confirmation in social interaction. The religious representation of the world absorbs
the social factor outside the human sphere in leitmotifs
like father, commandment, punishment, communication, word,
and love. Through theological generalization and dogmatization, this social factor is actually withdrawn from the
world. Extra-human sociality is banished into the form of
religion and is thus symbolically fixed. It is now only
related to the world; it is no longer *identical* with it[55].
The actual acting out of the religious myth in social
action, as for instance in the incest of the Egyptian royal
house, becomes superfluous. Or, if it does not become superfluous, it is shifted into a less consequential form like
the eucharist which can be practiced symbolically (no matter
how the theological dispute in this question is decided).

The de-socialization of the world both reduces the
social to human relations and expands the possibilities for
human social relations. A prerequisite for this development
is that the *selectivity of action* must to a certain extent
become visible and must be *attributable to individuals*.
This in turn is only possible if the structures of the societal system and its horizons of meaning produce a surplus of
possiblilities in the light of which all action can appear
as contingent. Only when it is clear that action is a
choice from a multitude of possibilities, does one need to
ask about motives[56]. Only when it is clear that a different
action could have been chosen, must one imagine the other as
an individual. For the individual is a constant point of
reference within the selection process, within the range of
possible selections, and within the limits of the reality
that has been chosen as the background of action. The individual as constant point of reference is a necessary supposi-
tion if action is assumed to be a selective process[57].

Furthermore, once this is assumed, anxiety is individualized
as well[58]. This in turn makes it necessary to generalize
the religious means of absorbing anxiety so that it will be
suitable for different sorts of individuals.

The relations among individually and contingently selective people present such a contrast to nature that they can
be conceived as the specifically social. As a result, the
social and the human come to be the same. The consequences
of this convergence can be understood from three points of
view. *First*, this convergence allows a *more definite
differentiation of the societal system from its environment*.
Restricted to relations among human beings, the system of
society distinguishes itself clearly from other societies
and from nature or the supernatural. Social relations are
now human relations; and as such, they can be ordered and
modified in their own terms. Consensus, for example, can
become a decision-making factor if spirits, animals, fruits
of the field, and other things are no longer members of the
system.

Secondly, a new *humanization of society* corresponds to
this differentiation. The type of society now possible
concerns the human being as human being. However, humanization does not mean that people are better off than
before, and especially not that they treat one another
better. Religious wars, the burning of heretics, etc., are
evidence for rather than against the connection between
humanization and the development of religion. For these
things happen precisely because people consider each
other—and can negate each other—as people, namely as
self-selective systems of action that are basically similar
to one another. This view of fellow human beings is also
why later development necessitated a greater differentiation
between social systems and personal systems. Such differen-

tiation was at first structural and then also theoretical.
It is required whenever the risks of humanity become unbear-
able.

The same theoretical context makes the *third* point of
view plausible. Only the religious de-socialization of the
world make *independent objective and temporal dimensions*
possible. These two dimensions not only became largely
independent of one another but also *independent of the
social dimension of meaning.* To put it into the most abstract formula: the ability to negate is gradually differentiated; it is relieved of social implications when the negation is temporal or objective.

There comes a time when important social processes
(e.g., political or ceremonial ones) are no longer
experienced as religious in themselves. Rather it may become the *responsibility of politics* or the *responsibility of
individual behaviour* to concern itself with the harmony of
the cosmic-religious and earthly orders. Such a shift gives
rise to new problems. First, there will arise the possibility of *consequential misbehaviour* and of failure.
Second, events can be *attributed* to either the divine will
or human misbehaviour. This *double* possibility takes
account of the first-mentioned contingency. Third, one can
expect a new consciousness of time as the dimension of event
and success, of crime and punishment. Effort can become a
variable quantity in such a dimension[59]. This change by
itself does not remove religious symbolism from the realm of
myth. However, religious symbolism must now relate to the
conditions that allow this kind of contingency. That is, it
must be abstracted so that it becomes compatible with a
variety of circumstances and with systems that can be in
more than one state.

Because of this demand, various models for the recon-

struction of contingency were tried out in early Near Eastern religions. The ancient Babylonians tried to solve the
problem by means of a pantheon, whose lack of moral obligations allowed it to be terrible and arbitrary, but not
entirely capricious[60]. On the way to monotheism, this
pantheon first became hierarchical and moral. The highest
God could now be identified with the moral principle (something which presupposes organized justice on earth). The
development continued above all in the subsequent Hebrew
religious tradition[61]. The Hebrews adopted the idea of a
communication between God and his people. This communication was contingent, historical, and variable in content!
As such, it was compatible with good and bad action, with
fear and hope, reward and punishment, and the fortune or
misfortune of Israel. This gave it stability in relation to
the changing circumstances of history[62]. Along with this,
another problem arises. Time must become more than concrete
phenomena that relate to the absorption of disappointment,
phenomena such as birth and death, generation and decay.
Time must be conceived as a *meaning-relationship* between
temporally distant events of the past and future. It must
also be seen as the space in which communication develops.
That is, it must be seen *historically*. For this way of
thinking, history is the history of decisions to which God
responds accordingly[63]. It is reflected as dialogue with
God[64].

The succeeding developments can be understood by study-
ing the history of the principle of causality[65]. The
specifically modern use of idealization and technology could
only be developed from this basis. Something similar holds
for that transformation of time-consciousness which sees
time as content-neutral linearity and as strict, irrevers-
ible differentiation of past and future. For all these

changes, Christian theology has played the role of midwife
and offered transitional formulae. This is especially the
case with the concept of creation which, in its absolutized
form, allows causality to become contingent. It is also the
case with the concept of time which is seen as having two
levels. On one level, time is still an eternal present;
that is, it is the (social!)[66] presence of God. On the
other level, time already allows progression by the continual changing of past into future[67].

Nevertheless, the modern era brought with it substan-
tial changes in the socio-structural conditions that make
these perceptions possible. Time has lost its last social
characteristic, the communicative presence of all times in
the present. Either this or it has replaced this characteristic with the mere possibility of "presenting" the temporal
horizons, past and future[68]. In this sense, an open time
has developed from a closed time. For this open time, history determines itself. History proceeds out of an imme-
morial past into an open, decidable future. It is no accident that, parallel to the establishment of this new temporal structure in the eighteenth century, humanism emanci-
pated itself from its religious foundation and sought to
legitimate itself strictly in its own terms[69]. To this end,
both optimistic and pessimistic variants were offered. For
the time being, this alternative did not let the question
arise, if it is at all meaningful to see the ultimate orientation of the human being in the human being himself.

It is certain that the extent of differentiation
between the temporal dimension and the social dimension
depends on the structure and evolutionary state of the societal system. In this respect one cannot return to a religious dogmatics that presumed a lesser degree of differentiation in its concepts of God and the human being. How-

ever, it may be possible to understand the consequences of
the attained differentiation better and to find more adequate semantic correlates. The evidence is increasing which
indicates that societal evolution has surpassed a state in
which it made sense to refer social relations to human
beings. In recognition of this situation, more recent
systems theories have often made the admittedly controversial assumption that a person, in the sense of an individualized personality, must be regarded as part of the environment and not as an element of social systems. The person
would therefore also be environment of society and of the
religious system. This assumption continues the specification of the social beyond the mere de-socialization of the
extra-human world. Personal systems are now differentiated
from social systems in the sense of interdependent system/en-
vironment-relations. Here lie perhaps the most decisive
consequences of more recent systems theory for religious
dogmatics[70].

                                         VII

     All analyses that use systems theory must take a plural-
ity of systems as their points of reference. The external
differentiation of society through the acquisition of
well-defined limits for a specifically human social system must be distinguished from the internal differentiation
of this societal system. In particular it must be distinguished from the differentiation of a special subsystem for
religion within society. It is to this latter that we now
turn. Even the functional differentiation of religion is an
evolutionary process of system-construction. Religious
dogmatics is its outcome.

     In comparison with the contemporary situation, it is
immediately evident that in pre-modern societies, religion

is clearly still relevant for society as a whole. For all
functional and media spheres, it still offers a kind of
basic security and variation barrier. It is this protec-
tion, after all, which makes the differentiation and
technical independence of these spheres possible in the
first place[71]. Above all political authority is legitimated
religiously. Thereby, its actions are limited by norms
which it itself has not created. The contingency formula,
scarcity, that is, the restrictive interdependence of economic need satisfactions, has its validity grounded religiously. For example, it may be seen as brought on by the
breaking of one of the deity's commandments(!) In this
case, the religios-moral requirements for behaviour under
the fundamental condition of scarcity can be explained as
well[72]. The functional and media spheres structured by
contingency formulae are not yet autonomously institutionalized. Although the full autonomy of individual media
spheres is already conceivable, it cannot yet be realized in
practice. Instead, such a possibility is described in
morally negative terms[73]. The extent to which independence
can be achieved depends on the degree to which the
differentiated subsystems can handle the risks involved. It
also varies from society to society and from medium sphere
to medium sphere. However, even with a high degree of
independence, the interpretations of the world given by the
individual media and above all their connection and mutual
support are mediated religiously[74]. Not uncommonly, this is
done by religiously duplicating the already differentiated
media codes, for instance, for truth, love, political power,
and reinterpreting them towards a unified world-view.

Even in earlier societal systems, the religious functions must meet requirements that perforce lead to the external differentiation of particular, specialized organiza-

tions. / At first this occurs only in certain situations,
leading by increments to the specialization perhaps of
certain cultic acts.   Then the differentiation is
accomplished through role differentiation and finally by
means of permanently functioning subsystems for specific
religious functions.   For the central function of ciphering
indeterminate and establishing determinable complexity,
society relies on one of its subsystems among others: on
the priests organized into temples and churches.   This reliance results in peculiar discrepancies and systemic disloca-
tions that produce techniques for bridging this difference
between whole and part[75].   "Do not interpretations belong to
God?   Tell them to me, I pray you" (Gen. 40:8).   Perfection
must be administered no matter where it arises because normally it is not self-evident.   Therefore, with all dogmatic
formulations one must always also ask what they mean for the
profession.   This reference to problems of practice is part
of the structure of dogmatics[76].   Presumably, a priestly
practice concentrating on the production or prevention of
certain effects can only be institutionalized with reference
to a very few, relatively simple problem-situations.   Disappointments are then interpreted by assuming the existence of
opposing powers.   It is a different matter when situations
involve more complex causes, are more transparent as regards
action, and have retroactive effects in the social system.
In these cases the danger of failure grows, and with it the
necessity of concealing failures as well as the necessity of
concealing concrete intentions.   This trend continues until
cultic forms are developed which no longer require the intention of a concrete effect and which are compatible with both
success and failure[77].   To maintain this distance between
performance and effect, interpretations require both professional co-operation and a new style.   These developments, in

turn, contribute to the further differentiation of the religious system from the rest of society.

At the same time, such external differentiation leads
to unfulfillable expectations because the foundations of
meaning specific to the system are easily "overdrawn."
Within the religious system, possibilities are produced and
formulated for the entire society which are not possibilities for the society as a whole. That is, they cannot be
accommodated within society. A differentiated societal
system creates more possibilities than can become actual.
This is an aspect of the above-discussed correlation between
differentiation and generalization. To take an example, in
medieval theology serious discussion took place as to
whether one had to wish the death of one's own father, if
God so willed it[78]. Thus unrealistic expectations emerge
for other subsystems, in this case the family, which these
cannot adopt as their own but can only treat as external
data[79]. The societal system is thereby put in a position in
which it can and must be *selective* about its *own* religious
expectations. This indicates a tension which can be seen as
a problem resulting from the evolutionary differentiation of
society. Within the religious system this problem can be
solved in various ways. The conduct of life can be strained
or stylized towards the ideals presented in the dogmas. One
can use tactical tricks like moral casuistry. Certain aspects of professional practice can be concealed; and there
are other ways besides.

In the light of these considerations, one may hypoth-
esize that a stronger *external differentiation* of the
religious system must lead to a greater degree of *dogma
construction* and to *ecclesiastically organized respecification* of these dogmas. This latter supplements or even
more or less replaces a ritualistic practice of religion.

The more a religious system is differentiated from society,
the less it can rely for direct support on the other functional spheres of that society. For example, it can no
longer take for granted that the brave and the warlike go to
heaven, or that what is good for the family will also please
God. The conditions necessary for the attainment of religious goals and salvation are separated from the conditions
for success in the other functional spheres of society. The
independent religious ideas are now only selectively
co-ordinated with these other functional spheres, for example, from the point of view of caritas[80].

The religious system in this case is widely separated
from the surrounding society and relates to that society
selectively, on the basis of its *own* premises. Yet it
remains relevant for the society as a whole. This state of
affairs is reflected in internal requirements. If the religious system takes on a *specific* and yet *universally*
relevant function, it must also switch internally from
primarily segmentary to functional differentiation. For the
demands on the religious system can no longer be met
adequately on the basis of system-construction that divides
segmentarily, into many equal or similar units.

In this respect, the late Roman phase was decisive for
the development of the West. If it did not effect this
restructuring, it certainly made it possible as an inchoate
historical process. The Christian movement successfully
avoided relegation to the status of one cult among others.
That is, it avoided incorporation into the still predominant
segmentary differentiation of the religious system. At the
same time, it was able to maintain its universal claim to
validity for all human beings. In this situation it had to
proceed almost as the enemy of religion, or in any case as a
political anomaly, different and intolerant. *At the same*

time, success depended on the appropriation of the already highly developed political and legal universalism of Rome. Augustine's doctrine of the two cities reflects this problematic, not least in that it cannot conceive these cities clearly, or differentiate them in a logically and morally unambiguous (i.e., binary) way.

The religious system of late antiquity does not end up abandoning the structural principle of segmentary differentiation. However, it reduces it to a *merely organizational principle* of a unified church of one faith. That is, the ecclesiastical organization takes the form of regional segmentation into bishoprics and parishes. As a result, a strictly *hierarchical* organization becomes necessary to correlate unity and regional segmentation. This hierarchy also acts as the differentiating point of contact with the outside society, especially with its equally hierarchical political system[81]. All this requires a *functional differentiation of the religious system into specifically organizational and specifically religious processes*, a differentiation that results in constant problems for church politics[82]. These problems stem at least in part from the fact that the differentiation of organizational and religious processes cannot in its turn be a purely organizational differentiation. Today, more than ever, developments in religious dogmatics occur outside the church organization.

Under the above-discussed societal conditions, the functional specification of the religious sphere can no longer be based primarily on the kind of ritual that is performed only at certain times and is timed so as to be compatible with various different actions before and after. This would allow an increasingly differentiated religious system to become irrelevant to society. Rather, greater

external differentiation requires greater generalization of
society's integrative methods.

Under the circumstances, *the religious centre of grav-
ity shifts from ritual to overarching questions of faith*
which must be dogmatized, interpreted, and exegetically
respecified[83]. The dogmas of faith assume a function in the
code of a particular communications medium which overlaps
differentiations within the system. The amplitude of myths
and explanations which was normal and harmless in older
religions based on ritual and cult[84], is no longer tolerable
if religion is based on more highly generalized symbols.
The correct understanding of faith can and indeed must become the subject of controversy, the settling of which spurs
the further development of dogma. This is a good time to
have a "book"! But no matter what path dogmatics chooses,
disintegrating effects must be tolerated since society can
now only be integrated on more abstract levels of institutional and symbolic compatibility.

De-ritualization implies above all that *greater
differentiation of expressive and instrumental processes*
becomes possible in the religion itself and in its social
relationships. A pronounced separation of love affairs and
financial affairs would be an example. In their execution,
rites are so concrete that expressive and instrumental (to
be sure, consciously manipulative!) functions fuse and are
interdependent[85]. To the extent that the "leadership" in
the religious system transfers to dogmatics, this makes a
greater separation of expressive and instrumental functions
possible. Dogmatics thereby becomes more compatible with
societal differentiation. However, it must also construct
and interpret symbols which reintegrate expressive and
instrumental processes into a unified conceptual scheme.
The primary differentiation is no longer, as in archaic

societies, a differentiation between the roles of the priest
and the people who take part in the cult at a distance. It
is now a more abstract differentiation of action by priest
and believers, *insofar* as this action fulfills religious
functions.

Even when religion can no longer be conceived mainly as
ritual, a distinct differentiation of the religious system
from society remains indispensible *even at the level of
cultic action*. In none of the important religions have
ritual forms of cult been fully discarded. For example, in
the first centuries of our era, Christianity was able to
leave its dogmatically generalized symbols open to the influence of the environment and cultural stimuli. The independence of a specifically Christian cult was an essential
prerequisite of this ability. With the growing strength of
the ecclesiastical organization, these tendencies even
increased. First the distinct cult and then the distinct
organization provided Christianity with a vital basis for
its own security. Without this, it would scarcely have been
possible to adopt and assimilate the thought traditions of
heathen antiquity to such a high degree. And the appropriation of these traditions gave a certain continuity of evolutionary achievements. Thus for instance, it provided for
the continuation of the partly monarchical, partly city-
state political terminology, of legal thought, of logic, and
of the general improvement in argumentative awareness.

Systems theory can, along with Talcott Parsons, de-
scribe such a development as a correlation of *increasing
external differentiation and increasing internal differentiation* of society's religious system[86]. In such a process,
both the level and the principle of differentiation are *more
strongly generalized*. Buddhism still clings to the level of
ritual for both external differentiation and internal differ-

entiation. Thus monks are contrasted with lay people and
meditation is separated from the earning of merit[87]. By
contrast, a stronger shift from ritual to belief and the
more abstract ecclesiastical form of external differentiation demand a different kind of problem-solving. External
differentiation loosens the functional association of religious and secular action to such an extent, that differentiation within the system must proceed along other lines.
Specifically, the internal distinction is now between cultic
action and charitable social action approved by religion.
This internal differentiation can no longer, like the
Buddhist one between meditation and the earning of merit, be
uniformly ritualized. The correlation between internal and
external differentiation now makes generalization necessary
in *both* respects. This generalization is accomplished by a
unifying development of dogma. One unifying idea with this
function is that the *same* God should be *worshipped* and *loved*
in the other person. This *horizontal* differentiation of
such different ways of acting requires a corresponding development in the *vertical*, namely, the development of symbolically generalized means of control and integration *above* the
level of cult and social action. The subsequent Reformation
shift from cult to communication is perhaps the most remarkable structural and dogmatic adaptation to this development.
And this in turn is only possible if the religious
system—again along the path of internal differentiation—develops a special managerial and administrative
organization on whose *action* no special religious demands
need be made because it serves religious *purposes* and
confesses religious *belief*[88]. Once this has been done, an
organized social system, the church, can become responsible
for the external differentiation of the religious system and
for the ability of its dogmatic development to maintain

cultural contact. /

In this way, functional differentiations develop gradually within the Christian religious sphere and are even
able to survive the re-segmentation of this religion that
resulted from the division into denominations. On the one
hand, *specifically religious communication is the functional
sphere of the bureaucratic church.* Here the religion
remains tied to ritual. However, in the new context of a
religion based on belief, the meaning of such ritual must be
understood; it must be theologically acclimatized.
Accordingly, the Christian sacraments are conceived as chan-
nels of grace or as signs of proven grace. Parallel to the
ritual, there are *charitable duties* that connect the church
with other sectors of society. But these duties do not make
grace superfluous: They do not allow salvation to be
attained solely by way of merit. In other words, the theology of grace prevents the dissolution of religion into mere
achievement. Theology defends the functional core of religion, its "proprium," from the constantly increasing
possibilities for commitment in the environment. The
doctrine of justification is a central tenet of theology
that is developed in this regard. Its existence points to
the need for a third kind of orientation, a third kind of
process. *Theological reflection* looks after the identity
and systemic interests of the religious system with the
required degree of consciousness and precision.
Elsewhere[89], we have designated these three incongruent
tasks as function, performance, and reflection. Function
refers to the relation of the system to the overarching
society; performance refers to the relation of the system to
other subsystems of the society; reflection refers to the
relation of the system to itself. In an externally differentiated religion based on belief, these three concerns can no

longer be attended to and represented by different gods with
different jurisdictions. Rather their justification and
harmonization become a matter for theological reflection
itself.

The coincidence of the evolutionary conditions necessary for such a total transformation is rare and unlikely[90].
From certain successful beginnings, only the Christian religion seems to have attained the extreme values in *all* the
designated dimensions: external differentiation, internal
differentiation, de-ritualization, dogmatization of faith,
and organization of methods for respecification[91]. The
"costs" of this achievement are perhaps only having to be
paid today. It would seem that the *genetic* significance of
Christianity for the liberation of those possibilities which
have produced modern global society is to be sought in this
peculiar combination. (As yet, this says nothing about its
viability as religion today)[92]. The decisive *historical*
causes in this case have yet to be investigated concretely.
They were decisive because of favourable sociostructural
conditions. Among others, one such cause might lie in the
fact that the *political* persecution and crucifixion of Jesus
of Nazareth was a negative factor in his own teaching that
could be interpreted religiously and, as such, could be
dogmatized as salvific event[93].

Besides this special and especially consequential exception, a certain external differentiation of religious practice seems to be a necessary condition for the establishment
and preservation of those higher religions that could develop dogmatics. This is not to say that religion can bear any
degree of autonomy whatsoever. Like the functions of the
economy, the polity, education and socialization, etc., the
function of religion is necessary. Both because of this and
because the religious function is of such central importance

for the constitution of the societal system, reservations
emerge at this point. External differentiation brings with
it a merely partial interpretation of the world; and this is
already no longer interpretation of the *world*. And abandoning the interpretation of the world is a first step
towards abandoning the societal function.

VIII

A functional analysis of religions and religious dogmatics must not only specify the systems which are being taken
as points of reference. It must also clarify the problems
towards which each of these systems refers. This consideration carries us one step further. Above (page 11) we already discussed the very indeterminate, almost tautological
character of a simple, general, and universally valid function for religion. Designating this function as the transformation of indeterminate into determinate or determinable
complexity for a societal system can only be a first step in
the analysis. It is not enough to say simply that religion
solves this problem and to leave it at that. On the contrary, this pervasive and basic problem emerges in various
societal systems in different ways. The structure of the
system as it were breaks up the problem and lets it arise in
different places in the form of special problems that are no
longer directly comparable. For this reason religion also
has important functions in regard to several structurally
dependent special problems. However, it only deals with
these problems as religion because they occur in the context
of the general determination function, because they con-
cretize this function. They can therefore be solved using
multi-functional and generalized symbols that can be applied
in a variety of ways. We shall demonstrate this with the
help of two selected examples of central importance.

1. Since the publication of Arnold van Gennep's famous
work[94], the use of magical, mythical, and religious ways of
transferring persons out of one status into another has been
recognized and investigated. Such rites of passage relate
above all to the age-related transitions in life, inclusive
of the limiting cases of birth and death[95]. Transition
rituals help to overcome orientation difficulties by offering univocal, often drastically illustrative substitute
orientations. These include extraordinary rules of action
for the transition period. Non-religious functional equivalents for such rites of passage have developed in modern,
highly differentiated societies in which transitions have
become everyday events[96]. Why and under what conditions
must religion solve this special problem?

The basic condition seems to be that a purely temporal
break is not enough to clarify the situation. The transitional state cannot be defined by differentiating what was
valid before from what is valid after because identity must
be preserved during the exchange. The transitional state
suspends the determinations of before and after. The person
to be transferred is "both...and" or "neither...nor," and in
fact simultaneously! His or her identity becomes unclear
and indeterminable. This situation raises the problem of
the determination of the undetermined *without presenting it
as a problem of the world*. A relatively concrete solution
is therefore possible. One might perhaps remove, simulate
the absence, or paint the transitor for a period of time; or
one might take the occasion to initiate the candidate into
the mysteries of the invisible and the unfathomable[97].

When the foundations of society change, the presup-
positions as well as the possible solutions for the problem
also change. More highly differentiated societies can provide social relations for *every* change which outlast the

change and support the identity. An example would be a love affair during the time of entrance into a profession. Closely related with this is the ability of these societies to offer a sharper and more abstract differentiation between world and time. As a result, the problem of transition can be articulated by a purely temporal break which as such does not put the identity and the determinability of the before and after into question. Thus the transitional situation loses its anomalistic and indeterminable character. Instead, it becomes just a "difficult" situation, a matter of co-ordination and learning difficulties that can be solved[98].

As a result of the increase in societal complexity and differentiatedness, religion no longer has to create very concrete definitions for transitional situations. Religious symbolism can be abstracted and dogmatized to a greater extent. However, it becomes all the more difficult to bring the function of religion to bear in this special problem area at all. Those changes of status that are especially associated with the religious system continue to be interpreted religiously. Examples are baptism and communion/confirmation[99]. For the rest, religion restricts itself to the role of a "helping hand" that is only called upon in certain situations and that is no longer functionally necessary on the level of society as a whole[100]. This helping hand is made available when the situation, although not anomalously, threatens to overtax the individual for whatever reasons[101]. The concept of "help" means that the transitional process itself is not a religious performance. Rather it means that only the action which interferes with the process from the outside is being religiously motivated or at least legitimated.

2. Our second special problem does not refer to change

but rather to the disappointment of expectations which are
closely linked with a situation or a position. A healthy
person becomes sick, a house burns down, a father does not
behave like a father. Such disappointments are an unavoidable aspect of the formation of structure. They present a
twofold problem according to their temporal relation to the
event.   Insofar as disappointments are anticipated as
possibilities but cannot be foreseen, they produce *anxiety*.
Insofar as they occasionally happen in fact, they produce
insecurity as regards the validity of the concretely disappointed expectations. Anxiety concerns the problem that
disappointments of determinate expectations are indeterminable; insecurity concerns the indeterminateness of
expectations that, in the light of determinate disappointment, should have been valid. Under certain conditions,
religion explains and absorbs such disappointments in *both*
respects[102].

A disappointment is more than an unexpected event. It
attacks the expectation itself, endangering the determination or determinability of future experience and action as
well. Also, to the degree that the expectation is generalized, other kinds of situations are similarly affected.
Disappointments reveal weak points in the structures, points
at which indeterminable possiblities can penetrate. Far
reaching anxiety and insecurity can be the result. In response to such a generalized threat, it is therefore reasonable to introduce generally applicable religious symbolism
to deal with these situations. The connection with the main
function of religion, the transformation of indeterminate
into determinate or at least determinable complexity, is
obvious.

Nevertheless, even in the earliest societal systems,
not all the ways of perceiving and dealing with disappointed

expectations were religious. In principle, there are two quite opposite ways of processing a disappointed expectation. One can *change* the disappointed expectation, substitute another for it, that is, learn; or one can *maintain the expectation contrafactually* and attempt to enforce it[103]. Each of these two strategies is subject to its own special conditions. And to the extent that the kind of disappointment-processing can be anticipated, the expectation itself takes on a colouring that is in one case *cognitive*, in the other *normative*. The expectation either anticipates something which is or something which should be.

The differentiation between cognitive and normative processes can be taken up in the structure of expectations and the alternative can also become a matter of choice. To the extent that this happens, the function of determination is taken over by predictable techniques for dealing with disappointments. The immediate reference to religion recedes. Even the earliest societies had non-religious, cognitively structured spheres of experience and action for direct dealings with nature. One can also find juridical normativity which is more or less well developed technically and is not experienced as a component of religion[104]. Whenever such cognitive or normative expectation-structures become differentiated, religion withdraws from the immediate business of absorbing disappointments. Instead, religion assumes the function of interpreting and legitimating the expectation-structures themselves[105].

Whether cognitive or normative, these domains of expectation become more extensive, more precise, and more distinguishable in the course of societal development. The higher religions concern themselves mainly with interpreting the foundations of these domains. The dogmatics of these religions remain compatible with their societies if they perform

this task adequately. To the extent that the higher religions continue to contribute to the absorption of disappointments, this is done in a round-about way by concretizing and
denaturing the dogmatic material[106]. On the whole, however,
the development of the modern scientific (that is, cognitively determinable) world-view has decreased the need for
this kind of explanation even in the every day life of society. In the common sense world of every day life, those
expectations remain virulent which are broken so rarely that
neither a cognitive nor a normative style of disappointment-processing is developed. In the more severe cases,
violations are still given religious interpretations until
society invents non-religious definitions even for these.
Thus, concepts of mental illness and the corresponding treat-
ments protect the normal patterns of expectation from
insecurity[107]. Rational theology can now only see a call
for loving care in the mentally ill, no longer a source of
inspiration or an explanation for unbelief. Eventually,
just as with transitional difficulties, only individual
problem-cases are left to ecclesiastical practice, cases in
which comfort and assistance can be administered.

What remains is the function of supporting the value
basis of the dominant expectation structures and of contributing to their consolidation. It would not make sense
simply to criticize and reject this function as such.
Nevertheless, it does become suspect and vulnerable when its
close association with the interpretation and abolition of
"costs," structural faults, and dysfunctions in the insti-
tuted structures is destroyed. It may be asked if that
organized "occasionalism" of care for the poor and disadvan-
taged, if caritas and diakonia, are sufficient counterweight
in this specific respect. For in the gulf between the
endorsement of values and the charitable treatment of prob-

lem cases (functions which, on their own, can also be fulfilled non-religiously), one loses the old unity of determination of the indeterminate.

The following insight is important for an adequate
theory of religion: neither one of the two partial functions—neither the bridging of change nor the bridging of
disappointed expectations—describes the function of religion adequately, and neither of these partial functions is
reducible to the other. On the level of dogma, this
situation results in ideas that encompass both kinds of
structural fault. On the level of religious theory, it
leads to a more abstract theory.

IX

One of the most important theoretical questions which
must be asked in connection with a functional analysis of
religion concerns the symbolic communications medium of
religion. Such a medium would be specialized for religion
and would be in the charge of religious professionals. In a
highly complex society, the function of religion can only be
fulfilled with the help of a communications medium that can
cope with special requirements. The search for a special
communications medium for religion replaces the older assumption that religion simply functions to direct social
motives[108]. As a result, it becomes easier to discern the
social conditions that make possible a special code for
religious motives and to distinguish this task from the
general problem of adequate social motivation.

On the whole, societal development presents a high
degree of congruency between subsystem formation and medium
formation. Politics works with power, science with truth,
the economy with money, the family with love. In all these
cases and above all in modern times, differentiation thresh-

re-interpreting media-codes.   What is the case with the
medium of religion?

     In the sociology of Talcott Parsons, "commitment"
functions as the media-concept to be inserted here, although
it is developed analytically in connection with the function
of   latent   pattern   maintenance   and   not   concretely   in
connection with religion[109]. The concept designates the
establishment   of   identity   by   the   reduction   of   other
possibilities,   but   does   not   offer   much   beyond   this[110].
Religious-dogmatic equivalents for commitment can be found
in concepts like confession, conversion, and baptism.   These
ideas express a selective self-identification (even if it is
the result of a "call") and are therefore only possible in
religions with a highly developed awareness of contingency.
However, self-selection is not a communications medium.   It
only reduces simple, not double contingency.

     If one considers communications with double contin-
gency, then the idea of a religious self-obligation must at
least be supplemented.   For instance, all communications
media have *code-rules against self-gratification*.   Prohibi-
ting self-gratification assures that the reduction of complexity   is   achieved   through   social   interaction.   The
reduction of complexity thereby attains greater selectivity.
In the case of love this is clear.   Further, one cannot
simply print one's own money; one cannot simply exercise
power by threatening with one's own physical force; and
truth is defined through its code as intersubjectively convincing certainty: the experiential evidence of the individual is not enough.   In the case of religious belief,
modern individualism has made it more difficult to institutionalize rules against self-gratification.   However, that
same individualism has also introduced the opposite and
polemical concept of "fanaticism"[111].   Originally, fanta-

icism meant the intolerant and stubborn adherence to private
insight sources in opposition to generally accepted beliefs.
That is, it meant self-gratification in matters of belief.

Moreover, the concepts of *inflation* and *deflation* can
be taken over from the general theory of communications
media and applied to the specifically religious medium. To
be sure, this part of the theory is only in its infancy and
has been conceived in very different ways. One can begin by
assuming that inflation and deflation belong to the specific
risks of externally differentiated and highly generalized
media-codes. One can further assume that they emerge with
all media, not just in the most familiar case of money. If,
as is the case here, one sees the function of media in the
transmission of selections, then both inflation and deflation can be thought of as disturbances of this function[112].
Inflation occurs whenever religion adopts a posture in which
the selections of alter (in themselves media-conforming) are
so abstract and so arbitrary that they can no longer appeal
to ego. Deflation occurs whenever religion adopts a posture
in which ego's range of selection becomes so concrete and so
lacking in alternatives that he can no longer process
alter's communications selectively. Thus, for example, a
theology of contingency and unrecognizable predestination,
but also a liberal "civil religion," could be characterized
as inflationary. A fundamentalistic theology by contrast
would be deflationary[113]. *Both* dangers are possible
depending on the code's degree of abstraction[114]. Both
dangers shorten the temporal horizon within which one can
confidently rely on the medium. Both dangers concern the
motivational capacity of the medium and can in extreme cases
lead to fusion with other media, that is, to the loss of the
advantages of media differentiation. Religious dogmatics
exist in part to control this problem. Failure in this

respect can lead to second-best solutions like an internal
differentiation between clerics and lay people or between
churches and sects.   Such a differentiation must then be
legitimated in the code of the medium.

Analyses of this sort presuppose that the concept of
belief or the concept of religious commitment is not defined
either psychologically, quasi-psychologically, or in any
other way with reference to the isolated individual.   Rather, either concept designates a code for processes of
communication.   Nevertheless, when considering the communications medium of religion, the feature of individual
self-selection still remains significant because it points
to a peculiar difficulty. *With other successful communications media, one can differentiate between experience and
action. It is questionable if this can be done with reference to religious self-commitment.* Since classical times,
religious experience has been *internalized*.   This internalized experience has been "subjectivized" in modern times.
Both these phenomena must be seen as *reactions* to the
differentiation of media within society.   They attempt a
greater separation of experience and action with greater
mutual indifference.   The problematic nature of this attempt
solution is obvious.   If self-commitment means definition of
identity for social as well as personal systems, and if
identity is always contingent identity-of-the-system-in-its-
environment, then the establishment of identity requires
attribution as both experience and action.   One cannot
select an identity for a system without at the same time
selecting a relevant environment and vice versa.   The binary
schema of attribution to either system or environment
already presupposes the constitution of the system in an
ordered environment.   It cannot be applied to the constituting processes themselves.

If this is the case, then the communications medium of religion does not follow the above-mentioned (page 19f) evolutionary trend of external differentiation on the basis of the attributive distinction between experience and action. If this is the case, then the religious sphere cannot develop a medium that uses only one type of transmission. It can therefore not attain a degree of specialization anything like truth or power and cannot tailor its symbolically generalized code to this type. Finally, if this is the case, then a very successful means for transmitting reduced complexity cannot be applied in the sphere of religion. This finding can be interpreted as evolutionary or cultural backwardness of religion; but it can also be seen as indicating that the functioning of religion is different when compared with other social mechanisms. This finding points to the problem of religion in a society that, in essential structural respects, is based on media differentiation. It does not however force the conclusion that there can be no specifically religious communications medium. It does say that a religious medium cannot be specifically devoted to the transmission of risky and improbable selections. Rather it must work at a much more fundamental level, making the practical experience of selectivity capable of being communicated as one that all have in common.

X

We can now ask if and how religious dogmatics can function adequately in the respects discussed. Let us repeat: we understand dogmatics in the broadest sense as those intellectual concepts which sort, process, control, and systematize religious experiences and situational interpretations. Sociologically, the concept also refers to a level of exter-

nal differentiation and self-direction of the religious
system as a subsystem of society. Religious systems take on
a form of dogmatic self-direction if societal development
demands from them a corresponding complexity and intellectual flexibility. This development implies something more
than the external differentiation of cultic action and religious interpretation of events (prophecies, interpretations
of dreams, etc.). Our question therefore becomes, how does
a religious system with dogmatic self-direction attain a
level of generalization at which it becomes structurally
compatible with the rest of society? (This question assumes
that the current problematic of religion is not to be found
in its inadequate "accommodation" to society, but rather in
its lack of structural compatibility).

     1. A first question concerns the *contingency formula*
of religion. In Western tradition, this formula is found in
the concept of *God*. Religious dogmatics is primarily
theology (and only secondarily religious doctrine, ecclesiology, etc.) because the intrepretation of the contingency
formula touches directly on the societal function of religion. The primacy of such interpretation in dogmatic systematization is a result of this direct connection.

     The shift from late archaic polytheism to monotheism
brought about a decisive increase in the abstractness of the
God-concept[115]. On a very concrete level, polytheism proved
quite clever and successful in developing religious contingency as the existence of "other" gods. Specific gods and
cults could be chosen for specific purposes. However, in
increasingly differentiated societies with more abstract
media codes, this solution to the problem of religious
contingency proved to be a mis-specification which was not
capable of further development. The monotheism which took
its place "de-socialized" the religious cosmos. It there-

fore brought about both a restructuring of the contingency
formula and a new level of generalization for religious
dogmatics—for dogmatics as theology[116].

The prototypical situation can be seen clearly in
Israel. The *oneness* of a tribal federation god who was
initially required for social cohesion, encounters an expanding awareness of time and is thereby confronted with the
changing history of a people in a politically and geograph-
ically precarious position. The result is generalization
pressure on the God-concept[117]. The God of Israel is
elevated to a *universal God* encompassing Israel and its
environment. This God then *chooses* Israel as his people of
his own free will[118]. At the same time, God is also disso-
ciated from time itself. Only this dissociation allows the
clear perception of events like the choosing of God's people
as promise and the birth of God in time as reconciliation.

"Accidental" conditions of emergence therefore create a
pattern that is stabilized through a higher degree of
abstraction. It thereby becomes compatible with a more
complex societal system. This compatibility is not restricted to temporal complexity. That is, the pattern is compatible not only with a succession of different kinds of
events. It is also compatible with the objective and social
complexity of subsequent societal development. The monothe-
istic God-concept prevails on this basis in the Roman
Empire. Here it is less a matter of temporal and more a
matter of objective and social identification. In this way,
the concept becomes independent of its conditions of emergence.

The greater abstraction connected with this shift is
easy to recognize if one considers it from the viewpoint of
a kind of "economy of symbols"[119]. Seeing connections
between different or preferably opposite things is an impor-

tant aspect of religious interpretation. It is easier to
make these connections if these different or opposite things
can be interpreted as being the same. Examples are birth
and death, taking and giving, becoming and passing away,
future and past, or quite and concretely, the dome and hol-
low of the hut, of the world-house[120]. By abstracting
towards the oneness of a creator God, the point is reached
where the different and the opposed are no longer explained
as the same, but rather through the same. Thereby greater
variety is permitted and logic is made possible.

A further significant result is the loosening of the
zero-sum principle associated with some of these
identifications. Thus scarcity is no longer a cosmic law;
rather, subject to the will of God, there is now the possibility of improvement—a theological licence for economic
improvement. Presumably one can also see the rejection of
the cyclical conception of time and the complete separation
of past and future during modern times in this context.

The formula, God, basically signifies the compatibility
of any contingency with a kind of supra-modal necessity. As
a result of this generalization, the task of respecification
becomes more difficult. All the contingency of an increasingly complex world, including evil and chance, must be
attributed to the one God and must therefore be interpreted
within the religious system. This requires a kind of
dogmatic generalization which, following Kenneth Burke[121],
can be described as perfection. The linguistic means of
intensification are extended and, ultimately with the help
of negations, stretched as far as possible. The negation of
perfection is blocked in the very idea of perfection. In
this way, a peculiar form of reflexivity is reached in the
sense that perfection protects itself from further exag-
geration. It always already implies the perfecting of per-

fection itself. According to its intended meaning, it thereby becomes necessarily non-contingent[122].

The intellectual techniques required to conceive of
perfection are thus of a negative character. In spite of
this, the non-contingency of perfection can be maintained
and can also be transformed down into something determinable. It is the limiting case in which a contingency formula can still work[123]. Above all Thomism, despite its
absolutized God-concept, succeeds in still accommodating the
problem of contingency. It does this with the help of the
distinction between primary and secondary causes, a distinction which is tailored to this problem and which is also
able to grant the domains proper to the world their own
relative right[124]. Because of this achievement, Thomism
became the dominant dogmatics of the Catholic Church.

To this one must add an important positive feature of
the Christian God-concept: his personality. The idea of
person functions to correct a problem that results from
highest perfection, namely the danger of its sterility. The
idea of personality makes believable that even the self-sufficient, unimprovable ens perfectissimum is interested in
the world and is inclined to give himself to it[125]. This
idea includes, among others, the assertion that God respec-
ifies himself. Thereby theological dogmatics to a large
extent avoids a problem that has become critical above all
in the fields of law and politics, namely that a highly
generalized code makes the selectivity of all respecifi-
cations visible and attributable. The turbulent history of
the councils shows that the mechanism does not always work.
In spite of this, the church never had to and never could
experience the kind of problems that might have *originated*
from its *own* selectivity, problems concerning sovereignty,
legal procedure, and democracy.

The idea of God as perfect person transforms indeterminate into determinable contingency, above all using the idea of creation and the understanding of contingency as "dependency on..."[126]. The idea that the world itself is contingent and a selection from a multitude of other possibilities becomes acceptable because the guarantee for the perfection of this selection lies in God as well. The concept of God explains and deactivates contingency to such an extent that contingency can be re-evaluated as a modus positivus entis[127]. Inversely, God so conceived can be proven as the expression of existence with the help of empirically experienced contingency.

Such a high degree of abstraction puts a great strain on the contingency formula. Evidence of this strain is found above all in the profusion of inner-dogmatic and church-political controversies during the high and late middle ages[128], in the necessity of retracting what is to be thought, and in the necessity of supporting, even morally and politically, the impediments to negation immanent to perfection. Finally, this strain encourages the formation of new forms of rationality for media spheres such as politics, science, and art, spheres for which an abstract theology had already, as it were, issued the birth certificates. The proof for God's existence seems to carry over to the ratio status, to the beauty of art, to economic success, or to the possibility of controlling the greatest world complexity with the minimum of conceptual means. At the same time, these new contingency formulae assert their own independence etsi non daretur Deus. In the religious system, a complementary reflection is blocked because reflexivity is absorbed in a God-formula that has carried generalization and perfection to the furthest extent possible.

Let us again look at how perfection ideas function.

They absorb contingency in that they flow back into themselves. Thereby they are suitable for the symbolic representation of relationships which we shall call *self-substitutive orders*. An order is self-substitutive if it cannot
be replaced by an order of a different type (e.g., truth
cannot be replaced by art, love not by power), but can on
the contrary only be developed further in the same type.
The most general self-substitutive order is the world, for
everything which could replace it must in its turn take the
form of world. The self-substitutive character of the world
is formally (simpliciter et universaliter) represented by
God.   Other self-substitutive orders such as truth, love,
art, and law have their own ideas of perfection which are
constructed analagously to the idea of God.   At the same
time, they all refer to the idea of God because every order
implies world.   In bourgeois society, this relationship is
broken in that a self-substitutive order begins to dominate
whose medium and criterium can no longer be conceived as
perfection: the money economy.   Belief in God does not
thereby automatically lose its meaning; but the idea of
perfection does lose its self-evidence. Money itself functions in a very different way. It is the perfect substitution within a self-substitutive order that is evidently
lacking perfection. Contingency can no longer be overcome
convincingly in universal or specific perfections. Perfection is therefore replaced in its function by the intrinsic
character of self-substitutive orders: the principle of
development. A theology which still deals with contingency
through the concept of God, which uses the (unanalyzed)
conceptual form of perfection, now finds itself opposed to
all evolutionarily oriented sciences, not least to sociology[129].

     What is left?   The assertion, God is dead, may have

been a consciously incongruous ciphering of the problem.
However, it still formulates the problem too theologically.
When compared with the modern development of other
contingency formulae, two things stand out. First, without
exception, since the end of the 18th century, there has been
a tendency to replace perfection with development. Then,
along with this, contingency formulae and selection criteria
become separated. The reconstruction of contingency for
important domains no longer provides selection criteria as
well. The contingency formula no longer serves as value at
the same time. By themselves, neither the binary schema-
tizations of just/unjust or true/false, nor the principle
of scarcity in economics, nor the formal legitimation
mechanisms of politico-juridical procedure supply criteria
or methods of decision-making. These functions
differentiate themselves in systems that respond to the high
complexity of the modern world. One of the advantages of
this differentiation is that a contingency formula cannot be
negated on the level of simple values. It is precisely this
differentiation which the religious system could not follow
under the direction of theological dogmatics. In the concept of God, two functions remain indivisibly merged, namely
the reconstruction of overt chaos into determinable variation and the regulation of selections. One should lead a
life pleasing to God and the diabolical components of the
highest principle are externalized. Today this may
be—similar to what we saw in the case of the communications
medium, faith—a comparatively atypical solution to the
problem. This need not, however, endanger its survival
capacity.

2. The importance and future of a religious dogmatics
do not depend solely on how the contingency formula is articulated. Another "necessary theme" concerns the *communica-*

tions medium of religion. This medium is that symbolically generalized code which controls the transmission of those selections that are considered to be religious. We have already been warned of the problem associated with this medium: religious experience and action cannot be differentiated. Religious dogmatics, and above all Christian dogmatics, has sought to meet this problem through the concept of faith.

The more precise definition of this concept fluctuates in at least two respects, on the axis of emotional to rational and in the extent to which faith is individualized as event or decision. Why religion thinks that its medium needs definition in these of all directions is something that would require further investigation. One reason may be that religion does not analyze its medium in terms of its function and therefore avoids the issue with psychological explanations that easily lead to misunderstanding. However, it is just at this point that dogmatics could arrive at a more unambiguous concept of faith by means of a sociological analysis and a comparison with other kinds of media.

When characterizing faith as a symbolically generalized communications medium, one point must first be clearly understood. The concept of faith is indeed central to theological dogmatics as is witnessed by the following: no true religion without faith, no justification without faith, no efficacy of the sacraments through grace without faith. However, even theologians find it difficult to conceive of religiosity exclusively as the possession and imitation of the right faith. This is especially the case with reference to Jesus' own conduct and speech[130]. There is a kind of practical immediacy to religious experience and action whose conformity to the faith need not be assured. Such immediate experience and action only become a matter of faith when

they become the subject of communication. This is especially noticeable with the founders of religions themselves[131]. Their behaviour cannot be conceived adequately
as practice of the faith. It generates faith in that it
occurs in situations where it is comprehended as communication and becomes the object of communication. For this
reason, theologically predisposed companions are necessary
in addition to the founder of the religion himself.

The linguistic code for faith must be generalized so
that it is open for a variety of contents. In general, this
is typical for generalized media. As little as money can be
specialized as a way of acquiring automobiles, or political
power as the punishment of criminals, so little can faith
consist in the observance of dietary laws or rules for
prayer. The differentiation of a special communications
medium for religion, namely faith, from media such as power,
authority, truth, love, or art is only possible with the
help of a symbolically generalized code. This differentiation therefore requires the development of a special
religious dogmatics. One must after all know, or find out,
or at least believe in the possibility of finding out, *what*
one believes. This gives the above (page 33ff.) discussed
association of external differentiation, de-ritualization,
dogmatization, and ecclesiastical organization its peculiar
relevance for the development of a communications medium
specific to religion. This association and development
peaks in the Christian religion and cannot be found anywhere
else in such sharp profile. One can say that, from a certain stage of societal development onward, a further external differentiation of the religious system was only
possible by means of the external differentiation of this
special communications medium. That is, it could no longer
be done by mere role differentiation. It therefore requires

that the conditions for such a medium-differentiation be fulfilled. In the final analysis, this external differentiation leads to where *faith can no longer even tolerate authority*. For authority is always supported by other social relations such as knowledge and the ability to express oneself, origins, prominence, etc.

Specific *risks* accompany a generalized symbolization which is based on external differentiation and is thus no longer of itself responsive to the problems of other spheres. These risks must be absorbed by the institutions. This is valid for all media and media systems. A characteristic example from the sphere of religiously specialized faith is the close and exclusive association of the prospect for salvation and faith, that is, the dogma of *justification by faith alone*[132]. Externally, this principle has the unequivocal function of differentiation. Internally, it is variable (and has been fundamentally changed in modern times) according to which action is regarded as the expression of faith. For example, the action of faith may be norm-conforming, cultic-sacramental, or it can be related to worldly attitude or success. The accommodation of faith to different situations is therefore mediated through changes in the relevance to faith of various actions. Viewed on the level of society as a whole, the dogma of justification by faith alone is always risky and can only be tolerated if the consequences of faith for society can to a certain extent be neutralized. The corrective can for instance by an overdrawn perfection (also functional for other reasons) of the faith code which makes faith a behavioural impossibility.

Thus far we have two consequences of externally differentiated generalizations, namely, risk and the need for respecification. The religious system responds to both of these with provisions which actually determine how the

faith-code is to be interpreted and what motivation there is
for the acceptance of selections. The possibilities and the
principle of justification for such provisions must also be
regulated in the code. The Enlightenment assumption, that
the humanity of human beings includes anything like a
natural and generalized religiosity, is hereby put into
question. Proof for this assumption is lacking right up to
the sociological difficulties of detecting such natural
religiosity through empirical research. It is more likely
that generalized faith can only be developed in conjunction
with these provisions for respecification and for the
absorption of risks. In our tradition these provisions took
on (but perhaps need not necessarily take on) the form of
organized churches[133]. When accompanied by a high level of
generalization, the supervision of the code and the prevention of inflation or deflation of faith[134] require a dogmatics in the sense discussed. Church (or its equivalent) is
therefore a dogmatic concept.

   Faith only acts as a communications medium if one can
assume that the one communicating believes. To the extent
that religion becomes a matter of faith, this assumption
must be demonstrable as well. This requirement becomes
especially evident in the history of the Christian faith.
It is fulfilled by a tradition of confessions and witnes-
sings in which believers attest to their faith, often under
extreme stress and therefore all the more plausibly. Or
witnesses attest to the fact that believers have attested to
their faith. In this context, it is remarkable how much
value is put upon physical presence and uninterrupted mediation, as if the medium presupposed communication among those
present as a security base[135]. Only in modern times is this
replaced by (translated and printed!) writing which has
always been called "testament." "If it weren't written, I

wouldn't believe it myself," attests Luther. Ultimately, the chain of witnesses leads back to the revelation of faith itself. Here it presupposes the self-revelation of Christ. The concepts of faith and revelation converge in the assumption that he believed in himself, that he himself believed that he was the Messiah[136].

The attested self-faith of the revealer provided the security base which made it possible to separate the communications media, truth and faith. Whereas truth has to be self-evident or be traceable to something self-evident, faith in the Christian tradition could be founded precisely on the non-commonplace, the improbable, the experience of strangeness, and on the historical contingency of revelation. However, consideration of the precarious motivational status of such a code prevented the drawing of the obvious conclusion: the admitted truth-incapacity of faith.

With the Reformation, the believer acquires a heightened awareness of individual self-selectivity. The independence (and thus the equality) of partners in a communicating, believing community is stressed[137]. The concept of faith is altered accordingly. Also, polemics against the institutionalized church were made necessary by the historical situation in which the idea had to prevail. That is, the de-institutionalization of the communications medium faith had to be advocated. However, this resulted in a misconception of the problem, partially because the concept of church as institution was too closely bound to the concept of organization. Communications media as such grow out of a problematic state of affairs, namely that reduced complexity can be transmitted even in communicative relations which exhibit two-sided selectivity and that a code to regulate these transmissions can nevertheless be institutionalized. This is especially easy to appreciate for truth,

love, and money. It is no different with faith. The fact
that the believer is now tuned to himself only accentuates
the conditions in response to which communications media are
institutionalized. The greater freedom of selection which
is to be expected with stronger system-differentiation and
with the abolition of multi-functional role combinations,
only forces a greater abstraction of the code that is to be
institutionalized. Perhaps this is what is meant when one
says that the Reformation replaced the visibly representative church with an invisible meeting of hearts in one
faith.

     The conception of faith as a code-dependent communi-
cations medium allows one to reformulate and answer the
controversial question, whether one must believe in dogmas
or whether faith is directed to what these dogmas designate:
God, Christ, the prospect of salvation itself. In this
form, the question depends on a conception of faith as
"visio" or "perceptio," or intentional experience[138].
However, the process of a communications medium is directed
first of all to the other with whom one is communicating[139].
Initially the other does not intend his own code but rather
communicates naively. The process can however become reflexive just like language generally and all media-directed
communication specifically. It can be applied to itself.
That is, it can include its own code in its thematizations.
Thus, for example, one does not talk about God but rather
about the correct concept of God. The faith process can
therefore "formulate"[140] the condition of its own possibility. The development of dogmatic theology presupposes that
faith has become reflexive, that holy words have a use beyond the liturgical setting. In a similar way, banks presuppose the possibility of financing monetary expenditures,
that is, credit; politics and public administration presup-

pose the hierarchical application of power to power; and positive legal systems presuppose that the establishment of norms can itself be made subject to norms[141]. Attaining reflexivity and solving the problems that result from it together constitute an important evolutionary achievement for all media and media spheres. This achievement makes the transition to modern society possible. On the other hand, whenever this possibility exists, one must avoid a situation where all communication problems become code problems.

With the help of reflexivity, the multi-leveled symbolization essential for all communications media can be realized. By this we mean the following: the code of a medium includes symbolically generalized rules that determine the possible combinations of other symbols. These rules direct the selection of experience and action. Without such multi-leveledness, communications cannot appear as information, that is, they cannot appear as selections from several permissible possibilities. Without such multi-leveledness, the degree of freedom and individualization possible for communications subject to any one code cannot be very high before the transmission of selections is endangered. Of all communication media, money has attained the clearest differentiation of level (and thereby the highest degree of freedom and complexity of permissible operations) because it distinguishes the practical symbols that circulate from the code that determines possible combinations. It can do this because quantities are clearly identified by means of minting and bookkeeping. Its example justifies the question of whether other media such as power or even faith cannot be institutionalized in a similar way.[142]

A look at the modern development of faith strengthens the impression that faith still exists as dogmatics but has largely ceased to function as a code for general social

processes.   Today dogmatic controversies only interest the
participants and a very limited public.   Thus, a danger that
is typical for other media, especially love and power, does
not exist for faith.   This danger is that too many communication problems become code problems.   For faith the opposite
is closer to the truth: code problems no longer affect any
communication whatever (except communication about the code
problems themselves).

This problematic situation cannot really be understood
if one maintains the traditional concept of faith and the
idea that the themes of faith are fixed by dogmas.   From the
point of view of dogmatics, this could mean that the concept
of communications medium is irrelevant to its proper
subject-matter.   The discrepancy can however be seen as
implying the opposite, namely that dogmatics must re-examine
its concept of faith.   If it is true that societal
development is determined or at least co-determined by the
differentiation of communications media, then the question
of a communications medium for religion becomes unavoidable.
Once this question has been asked, one can respond to the
idea that religion has limited possiblities for development
by comparing religion with the structures and functioning of
the currently most successful communications media.   For
such a comparison, the concept of faith would have to be
formulated accordingly.

The   motivational   problems   that   result   from   the
generalization of symbolic faith-codes are important.   They
are also essentially unsolved.   By motivation we do not mean
the demands of "internal" causes of action but rather,
following Max Weber, those reasons for a selection that are
understandable or are to be made understandable.   We mean a
state of affairs that is first and foremost linguistic and
social but which then, in a very complex and inexplicable

way, becomes causative in the psychic and organic systems as
well[143]. This concept of motivation makes it immediately
obvious that motives really only become necessary as a
result of generalizations and transparent selectivity.
Motives are thus not simply psychic causes of faith so that
there would be no faith if they were lacking. Motives are
also and above all the results of faith and the themes of
faith. They are these things in such a way that they can
become retroactively causative and can effect the acceptance
of selections[144]. The code of a medium must therefore also
produce and regulate viable motives. It must do this under
conditions determined by the state of the societal system
and thus more or less beyond the control of the medium.
Religious dogmatics must fulfill this function as well.
There is no certain guarantee that the motivational function
can be combined in all circumstances with the other
functions of religious dogmatics[145]. Above all, such a
guarantee cannot be derived from the "essence of religion"
or from the concept of faith. Today, for example, it is
doubtful whether "justification" is still an adequate
concept for the motivational situation in faith. Quite
aside from the question of what social conditions are
necessary for the development of religious motives, we are
still faced with another question. How complex and abstract
can a dogmatic system get and still expect both to interpret
contingency and create motivational formulae, while controlling both the inflation and deflation of faith?

3. Every symbolically generalized communications medium
must face the question, if and to what extent it can rely on
coding the conditions for the use of language as the sole
means of assuring communicative success. The actual physico-
organic presence of communicating partners provides additional motivational resouces but also brings with it certain

hazards and environmental restrictions.   The communicating
partners are present as systems that one can see and hear,
bump and stroke. They impose themselves in their physico-or-
ganic capacity and set insurmountable limits to every
communication[146]. This fundamental condition of communication is represented in the symbolic structures of the most
important communications media.   Symbols that do this can be
called "symbiotic mechanisms" because they refer literally
to the communal life of people[147].   A few examples will
provide sufficient verification of this thesis.   In the
domain of power, the reference to physical force seems to be
indispensable.   The same goes for perception in the domain
of truth and for sexuality in the domain of love, no matter
how much in each case the reference is put in the background
and minimized.   In a similar connection, Parsons speaks of
"real assets" as correlates of generalization[148].

     The failure of the attempt to reduce the security base
of faith to the communications of witnesses and to testi-
monies of faith is therefore not surprising.   This failure
leads to the following question.   Can rituals function as a
symbiotic mechanism after having lost their central place in
religion?   One must remember that the de-ritualization of
the faith-religions involved the spiritualization of primarily those rituals which proved to be the essential core of
religious communication.   And even physics was preferable to
anthropology in the search for an understanding of the
Lord's Supper.

     The title of sacrament vouches for the dogmatically
correct interpretation of ritual.   Sacraments are thought of
as mediations of grace.   For the middle ages, the realization of sacraments on earth touches on questions of causality.   The central problem is twofold.   On the one hand there
is the question of the extent to which the immediate effi-

cacy of God can be concentrated in the ritual. On the other hand there is the question of the extent to which this same efficacy can be stretched out over time so that a kind of depository of grace results which the church, under specified conditions, has at its disposal. This interpretation along with the use of physical categories like substance and quantity introduces an interpretation of ritual that ultimately no longer does ritual justice. As a result, innovative attempts to defend the dogmatic corpus in response to emerging problems of consistency are hampered because they affect the rituals. Looking back at the centuries of effort, it becomes evident that precisely at this point dogmatic harmonizations always produce controversies that sometimes even lead to schisms. It becomes evident that the possibilities for negation grow with articulation and that herewith (and especially with remystifications) the security function of the "real assets" of faith is lost. As the dogmatic interpretation of the sacraments proceeded, the meaningfulness of the immediate was lost. At least in the context of dogmatics, this could not be interpreted.

This becomes clearer if one takes into consideration the function of symbiotic mechanisms and also the function of those factors which prevent negation in the communication process. Along with Mary Douglas[149], one can ask if Christian preachers should not pay more attention to the function of the body as a social medium when it comes to de-ritualizing their religion. But a sociological statement cannot go beyond this recommendation. Functional analysis is after all anything but a technique for recovering immediacy.

4. If the external differentiation of a religious system such as the Christian produces exaggerated expectations for religious experience and action (see above, page 31f), then the relation of world, system, and environment

changes for such a system.   For us, environment refers to
that section of the world not attributed to the system;
world refers to the totality of the possible in the system
and its environment.   Religious systems of this kind, then,
with sharp distinctions between members and non-members,
inevitably discover that their *own members* do not meet the
expectations of the religion.   The chosen people of God do
not live according to God's commandments.   This experience
becomes strong enough to demand an answer if these expectations are formulated normatively as in the Hebrew tradition,
and not only "meritoriously" with a view to possibilities
for merits and salvation[150].   One can no longer react to the
syndrome of religious normativity and sin in the chosen
people with distinctions like friend/foe or near/far.   Later
prophecy reacts to the problem by combining the above-discussed (page 51) generalization of the national God to a
world God with a solution of the contingency problem through
an *eschatology*.   In other words, the solution is transferred
into the realm of time.   As a result, it not only has national characteristics, but also already universal ones[151].
This latter implication is symptomatic and can be treated
with the methods of systems theory.

     In this situation, religious dogmatics can no longer
manage with the simple positive/negative differentiation of
system and environment.   It can no longer fall back on the
idea that the members are good and the non-members, by contrast, bad.   That is, it can no longer reconstruct the world
as the totality of this polarity.   A defensive posture or an
indifference to a hostile environment gives no adequate
indication of how to understand the laxity of one's own
members or of their susceptibility to sin.   Christians even
have to tolerate community of the sacrament with the wicked,
hoping for a sorting out at the Last Judgment.   It is for

these reasons that the early Christians could not maintain their environmental indifference and their submissiveness. The relation to the environment had to be transformed into a relation to the world. *This new relation poses the question of the acceptance or rejection of the world, a matter that cannot be decided for structural reasons and is therefore postponed until the end.*

Moreover, situations can arise which reveal that the adversaries in a hostile environment also act according to their own rules of faith and moral points of view. The captivity of crusaders was one such incident which had far reaching consequences for the middle ages[152]. Even if there was only diplomatic interaction, the situation required generalizations that cut across the boundaries of faith. Once such generalizations were made, they could no longer simply be denied a meaningful basis and an approved order into which they could fit. Here again, the unity of faith, system, and world was dissolved.

No matter how it is brought about, thematization of the world means that totality can no longer be attained by *co-acceptance of the opposite.* Now totality can only be arrived at by *formulation of the unknown*[153]. This requires new forms of attribution. Above all, the expedient of accepting oneself and rejecting the environment is blocked. The "resemblances" of members and non-members become impossible to ignore[154]. Such similarities cannot be interpreted as an attribute of the system or as an attribute of the environment. They can only be attributed to the world[155]. People simply are subject to sin because they live in the world. Until the end of the world, the church remains civitas permixta[156]. The more sharply the differences both between system and environment and Christians and heathens are maintained, the more abstract must the concept of world

be which is still compatible with such differences. Ultimately, the difference between the just and the damned is
regarded as *unrecognizable* and therefore *becomes compatible
with every actual world*. Thereupon, the distinguishing of
the reprobi who are also believers demands *subjective*
reflection on the conditions that bring certainty of salvation.

Thus the structural conditions of this situation encour-
age the projection of a *universalistic concept of the world*.
The   concept   nevertheless   has   a   systemic   basis   and
corresponds to systemic problems. However, this does not
indicate what dogmatic material is available to give such
concepts   of   the   world   plausibility   and   motivational
capacity.   Because of its origins, Christianity could
reasonably resort to the temporal dimension, representing
world history as the sin and salvation history of both
heathens and Christians.   Thereby more inconsistency could
be tolerated in the objective world-view, making it possible
to reformulate the latter as a dramatic event which would
take on *successively different* states and terminate in an
eschaton.

However, for the sake of its function, a religiously
determined concept of the world always remains a reduction.
So is the Christian one also a reduction. To use the words
of Oskar Köhler[157], it is a representative presentation of
"world" in one's own world.   Until modern times, regional
societies selected determinable possibilities to produce
worlds which were always imagined as limited. In historical
retrospect, these worlds appear to us as "world-views."
contemporary global society incorporates such world views,
that is, it must imagine worlds in its world history. This
fact forces a world-horizon that is both reflexive (applicable to itself) and open to the future. The categorical

structure and determinability of this horizon will decide
the future of religion. Whence emerges the question to
which we will return at the end: can religious dogmatics
arrive at the concept of a *non-negatable world*?

5. The cases in which societal development leads to
the non-identity of political and religious reference groups
are relatively rare. When this does happen, the societal
function of religious dogmatics requires that it project its
own *concept of society*. With this concept, religious
dogmatics can set itself apart from the politically constituted societal system in which it finds itself. Yet the
concept cannot simply be a rival one on the level of politics (such as democracy vs. monarchy). Instead, a different
combination of characteristics must respond to the specifically religious function, resulting in a concept of the
perfection of human social nature. In the Christian tradition, this is expressed in the ambiguous idea of the *Kingdom
of God*. This idea postulates social solidarity in a form
which is based neither on kinship ties nor on territorial-
political ties. Rather it is indifferent to both of these.
Thereby religious dogmatics strengthens its independence
from concrete societal demands and increases the chances for
an independent development that allows it to survive even
when it has lost contact with society and become obsoles-
cent[158]. The reliance on political concepts such as civitas
or imperium shows that it is no longer possible to return to
the archaic clan unions that preceded the political constitution of society. For this reason, the religious concept
of society cannot simply be a negation of the political
concept[159]. The Church Fathers were well aware of how much
the politically stable peace of the Roman Empire was a condition for the expansion of the Christian faith and therefore
was the providence of God. The city-state terminology of

the civitas sine societas civilis influenced the terminology
of Christian dogmatics[160]. However the religious projection
makes a different kind of demand on human society. It is
neither a substitution for the political principle of societal constitution nor is it the opposite of this principle.
The necessity and systemic status of the differentiation
between *two* kingdoms is especially clear in the Christian
tradition in light of the fact that Jesus of Nazareth floun-
dered because the distinction was not evident enough. The
distinction is also expressed and stabilized in the dogma of
the *Trinity*[161]. This doctrine weakens the structural
isomorphism of the two kingdoms—there are no trinitarian
monarchies—*but does not abandon it altogether*. A sociological conclusion that follows from these observations is
that society can no longer be interpreted in its totality
from the political or from the religious points of view,
even though it is one social system. Naturally, this cannot
be the theological definition of the situation. In any
case, dogmatics still has the task of interpreting the Kingdom of God: what it is, where it is, whom it includes, and
when it is coming.

   Whenever politics and religion are more sharply differentiated, politics is relieved of its erstwhile role as
mediator between earthly and cosmic events. Religion now
claims this role exclusively for itself. This functional
loss gives politics greater freedom and the ability to define a specifically political responsibility. Earthquakes
and crop failures as such are no longer reasons for killing
the ruler. The functions of the ruler in ritual disappear
but he still concerns himself with the construction of the
temple. For its part, religious dogmatics still claims the
right to judge politics. However, the dissociation of political and religious criteria eventually leads to a situation

in which religion can only judge politics in terms of
whether or not it supports the ecclesiastical religious
system.

6. A highly developed religious dogmatics must also
interpret the external differentiation of the religious
system. External differentiation is not only a sociological
state of affairs, but also a theme of faith because it is a
condition for the possibility of advanced forms of religiosity. In our tradition, it is represented in the concept
of *church*[162]. One cannot believe in external differentiation; but one can believe in the church if one includes
some concrete contents and excludes a too abstract consideration of alternatives to church. Therefore, if the transition from sociological theory to religious dogmatics were
to be undertaken consciously, the process would have to be a
reduction of complexity: dogmatics would have to incorporate and develop ideas using an abstract systems theory as
a guide. External differentiation of the religious system
also presents ecclesiology with the task of describing the
relation between system and environment. Above all, ecclesiology must conceive the relation of the religious system to
a society in which it is only a subsystem and yet represents
a central function of the whole[163]. Themes such as "the
church and the world" or "the church and society" have their
origin here. To articulate this relation, dual schemata of
a very different kind are offered. Examples are
here/beyond, corporate body/organization, above/below, and
internal/external. All these can be interpreted as both
opposite and related[164]. Here, as elsewhere, paradoxes
serve to give dogmatics reserves of elasticity.

Religious dogmatics is justified in refusing to conceive of the church as organization[165]. Societal systems
and organizational systems are on different levels of system-

construction and fulfill different functions. Society is
the all-embracing system of communicative relations between
experience and actions. Organizations, on the other hand,
are systemic structures characterized by entrance and exit
requirements. From an evolutionary point of view, these
levels of system construction become more widely separated
with the development of modern global society and thereby
acquire their own distinct forms. The societal system loses
the organizational characteristics of the old, politically
constituted, territorial societies and at the same time
loses the direct regulative grip on the structure of individual organizations. Now its only influence on organizations is as their ordered environment. As a result, society
can depend more than ever on rationalized organizations that
relate to their environment. At the same time, society can
be an organization to a much more limited degree than ever
before. This holds true not only for society as a whole,
but equally for its primary subsystems: for religion,
politics, the economy, science, art, family life, and education. In all these cases, neither the general societal
functions nor the corresponding communications media can be
brought completely under the umbrella of a single organizational system. Moreover, precisely those structures with
which these subsystems respond to the very high complexity
of modern society cannot be regulated in an organizational
form. Examples of this situation are the incongruity of
politics and administration in the political system[166], the
market mediation of production and consumption in the economic system[167], the relationship between disciplines and
theoretical paradigms in the science system[168], and the
relation between home and school in the educational system.
The situation is not different in the religious system. To
be sure, it appears in a variant that is specific to the

religious function and subsystem. However, it is fundamentally in accord with the general insight that, in a highly complex society, general societal functions must be
repeatedly split up, reduced, and reformulated before they
can be transferred to the level of organized systems. The
fact that religion and the church cannot be totally organized need not be explained by appealing to the special qualities of things religious. Precisely for this reason, religious dogmatics has difficulty formulating this problem in
its concept of the church without also discrediting the
church as organization.

Almost from the beginning, the Christian churches were
organizations that could not be organizations only.
Although they have long experience with the problem, they
are not dealing with it adquately today. The old solutions,
above all considering the organization itself as sacred,
presupposed a relatively limited differentiation of the
systemic levels of society and organization. Because these
levels are currently more widely separated, these solutions
are no longer convincing. On one level they disturb the
effectiveness of the organization when for example "ordina-
tions" are regarded as career prerequisites. On the other
level, that of general society, the organization remains
over-articulated, incapable of reflection, and thereby also
incapable of representing the world and society religiously.
We shall return to this point at the end.

The churches attempt to absorb unorganizable societal
complexity with forms of differentiation peculiar to the
religious system. The subsystems for politics, the economy,
and science do something similar. First there is the differentiation of active and non-active members. This distinction cannot be organized because the membership requirements
of an organization can neither be applied nor not applied to

the latter. Then there is the differentiation between
organized action and religious communication. Today, this
distinction seems increasingly to be the topic of a self-sup-
porting discussion that is independent of church politics.

7. As we noted above (page 38ff), all religions are
confronted with the contingency of social status changes and
with their limiting cases, birth and death. The evolution
of society can result in an increased complexity and contin-
tingency of the world. Societal development can also
individualize the biographies and destinies of human beings.
If these two developments coincide, then a need arises for
assuring individual well-being that has become contingent
within a system where the dimensions of meaning extend morally, socially, spatially, and temporally beyond any particular situation. This uniform expansion of meaning is engendered by the social structure. Both this expansion and the
individualization of contingent destinies require an
interpretation. This changes the problem of status
changes[169]. Based on archaic rites of passage, advanced
religions develop a specifically religious thematic of salvation. Salvational interest, salvational expectations, and
the conditions for attaining salvation are formulated in the
light of a status change at the boundaries of this life and
are connected with the circumstances and events of life in
society. The idea of an undifferentiated and unavoidable
after-life for everybody is replaced by an idea that assumes
the contingency of salvation, an idea that admits an open
possibility and various states[170]. The after-life depends
not only on the direct and concrete circumstances of death,
but also on the more abstract criterion of conduct during
life[171]. Both conduct during life and the state of salvation are assumed to be contingent. That is, they are both
"also possible otherwise." However, they are also non-con-

tingently correlated. That is, they are linked through structurally invariant relations of the type, "if...then." This produces a theme of religious dogmatics that is necessary at this state of development: the interpretation of a *non-contingent relation of contingent states and events*. Based on *this form* of soteriology, religious systems can become crystallization-centres for relatively long term, institutionalized interests. Institutional developments in other areas can then support themselves on these interests. Further development therefore depends on how these interests are both formulated and endowed with motivational capacity.

We have already noted in passing (above, page 31f) that a stronger external differentiation of the religious system is accompanied by an abstraction of the themes of salvation. Upon closer examination, one must distinguish between a more abstract description of the *prospects* of salvation and the *conditions* or factors of salvation that are selectively emphasized by dogmatics. In *both* respects, advanced religions distance themselves from the commonly accepted social expectations[172]. They no longer have to tie the prospects for salvation to a good life, to say nothing of a well-appointed life. Also, the conditions of salvation are no longer immediately dependent on the fulfillment of familial, military, political, legal, or other obligations. Instead, they are reformulated from the viewpoint of dogmatic consistency.

There is thus a tension between the opportunities for dogmatic abstraction and the natural interests of the religious clientele[173]. The problems that result from this tension must be absorbed and processed in the dogmatics itself. Important ambivalences help to solve these problems. For example, in Indian religion, the mechanics of reincarnation offer a double possibility. One can either be

reincarnated into a better life that one can picture concretely, or one can be *transferred into a Nirvana that can
only be described negatively*. This double conception offers
something to everyone, no matter how sophisticated his/her
salvational interests are.   In Christian dogmatics, the
conditions of salvation have been discussed since classical
antiquity in terms of the relation between *merit* and *grace*.
Apparently it is difficult to do without either man or God
as factors of salvation.   This distinction also responds to
the need for differentiation within the religious system[174].
As a condition of salvation, merit correlates with the
performance-relationship of the religious system to its
societal environment and with the differentiation of society
that makes these relationships necessary.   As a condition of
salvation, grace, by contrast, correlates with the central
function of religious communication within the religious
system itself.

In the light of these correlations, it is especially
interesting to look at extreme solutions that take only one
of the two factors into consideration.   The most obvious
response is to lessen the risks of such onesidedness through
theological compromises.   That is, one replaces the instability of the extreme solution with the instability of a
combination that envisions the co-operation of merit and
grace.   The problem is then dissolved into theological
controversies that admit many different points of view[175].
The solutions that are offered rely to no small extent on
the ability of dogmatics to insert an agnostic factor.   For
example, it is assumed that karma is co-determined by behaviour before birth (that is, it cannot be remembered!).   In
the Christian religion, something similar is accomplished by
abstracting and perfecting the contingency formula, God,
whose knowledge and will remain unrecognizable[176].

Here again, rather important sociological questions can
be asked. For example, is it at all significant that Buddhism puts more emphasis on abstracting the states of salvation whereas Christianity puts more emphasis on abstracting
the *factors* of salvation? Presumably, this discrepancy
points to significant differences in the way these religious
systems were differentiated from society, differences in the
relevance of action in each system, and differences in motivational structure. Abstraction of factors seems to be the
more momentous of the two. It seems to require more presup-
positions but also seems to be a more effective engagement
of the social structure than an abstraction that produces a
merely negative conception of the state of salvation. This
brings us to the famous Calvinism/capitalism discussion
started by Max Weber[177]. The late middle ages and the
Reformation added a critique of merit and a radical shift
towards grace to the general Christian emphasis on the factors of salvation[178]. This radical shift emphasizes the
central function of religion at the expense of the concrete
performance-relationships with the societal environment. In
doing so, it presupposes that the other subsystems of
society, especially the family and the economy, can become
relatively independent from what is considered to be merit
in the religious system. Based on some very controversial
ideas, Weber assumes that this shift *created motives* for
rational economic and even rational scientific action.
However, what is more important is that the process *dismantled interferences* of religion in the economy and science
which had taken the form of relatively concrete evaluations
of action relevant to salvation. Then, with the beginning
of bourgeois society, the problem comes to be expressed in
politico-economic terms (most clearly in Hobbes). The evolutionary success probably lay more in the strong disentan-

glement and differentiation of systems than in the special
effectiveness of an ascetic motivation for achievement.
Therefore it was not that one sought a substitute for religious certainty of salvation in the economic sphere, but
rather that this was no longer possible.

Furthermore, if there is a relatively marked theological tension between abstract salvational themes and those
that are more related to concrete needs, does this not presuppose sociologically, *communication barriers* such as those
which exist in a society with well-defined social stratification? This assumption could explain why the Puritan tradition broke down so rapidly in the United States and why it
was replaced with a theologically undemanding and socially
eudaemonistic Civil Religion.

A final question concerns the importance of a doctrine
of salvation in religious dogmatics when compared with other
systemic functions. The interest in salvation functions as
the point of departure for the motivational mechanism of the
faith-code. To a degree, then, this interest must be formulated in the code of the communications medium. If the
relation of God and human beings is conceived primarily in
terms of salvation, then there is a primacy of media problems in the religious system. This is not self-evident. By
contrast, the concept of God, as the contingency formula of
the system, represents its own function, namely the determinability of world contingency. In the Catholic tradition,
this contradiction is expressed in a key theological controversy, namely in the different answers to the question, Cur
Deus homo?[179] According to the prevailing (above all
Thomistic) conception, the Incarnation of God was a reaction
to the Fall in the interests of salvation. This answer
stresses motives. Following Duns Scotus, the opposing
conception sees in this answer a limiting of the omniscience

and a conditioning of the free decisions of God. Both these
things must be rejected. This opposition sees the reason
for the Incarnation in the self-revelation of God, that is,
in a process of emanation and respecification of that which
functions as contingency formula. In the one case, the
medium has primacy; in the other, it is the contingency
formula of religion. Dogmatics has an option. It can direct itself to the motivational capacity of religion or it
can direct itself to reflective capacity and the world[180].
It is indicative of the evolutionary state of the societal
system that, even though an *alternative* is presented here,
the debate on this alternative can occur within the limits
of *one* church and *one* faith.

8. With greater external differentiation of the religious system, *time and history* emerge as further necessary
themes. We showed this in section VI. The differentiation
of the cosmic and earthly orders symbolizes the external
differentiation of the religious system. It thereby allows
events in time to be perceived as contingent. It also makes
meaningful relations between temporally distant events
necessary. On the other hand, the societal system does not
yet change its structures so quickly and so regularly that
everyday orientation would imply knowledge of a different
past and a changing future. One can still manage with
limited temporal complexity, that is, without significant
qualitative differentiation of past, present, and future[181].
The biblical idea of time, for example, responds to these
pressures by conceiving history in terms of its extremes,
the beginning and the end. This response makes it possible
to judge the meaningful coherence of the whole without
differentiating the in-between time all too much (as for
instance modern theories of evolution do)[182]. An earthly
time spans between the Fall and the Last Judgement. Al-

though this earthly time is divided into epochs, it can
nevertheless be grasped as a moral continuum and as a unified history of salvation. As time, such a history relates
to the beginning and the end, to the Fall and the Redemption, as *presents*. That is, it does not permit a complete
differentiation of past, present, and future[183]. In addition, the Christian can see the guarantee for the future in
the presentness of a past event within history. That is,
he can understand the unity of the history of salvation as
something that happens within time[184].

A time that spans from the beginning to the end and
that is determined by these extremes can already be conceived in a certain sense as linear. Linear and cyclical
ideas of time were developed *side-by-side* in Egypt[185]. This
side-by-side seems to have persisted in both the Greek and
the Hebrew understandings of time. The experiences and
actions available in these societies did not have to be so
co-ordinated as to require a decision for only one or the
other of these ideas, at least not at this level of abstraction. Many theologians and philosophers distinguish between
Greek (supposedly cyclical) and Hebrew (supposedly linear)
concepts of time[186]. But even the textual traditions do not
justify such a contrast[187]. However, especially in the
Christian tradition, there were definite reasons for not
applying the literary and dominant cyclical concept of time
to history[188]. Indeed, this would have meant that even the
Passion of the Lord could be regarded as a regularly recur-
ring event. This would have eliminated the profundity of a
salvific event that could only happen once and that was only
necessary once[189]. As a result, a linear idea of time
became necessary at least for the conception of history.
Moreover, the linear idea of time allows the ambitious and
improbable thesis of a unique revelation[190].

Accordingly, the Christian cleansing rituals, namely baptism and the eucharist, differ sharply from predecessors which were associated with changes in the season, such as the celebration of the New Year[191]. The Christian rituals are also seen as periodic re-enactments of a past salvific event[192]. They can therefore only be made plausible in a society that can also think cyclically. However, they are themselves no longer bound to the temporal rhythm of a cycle. Rather they can be re-enacted *at any time* in a linearly progressing time. As a result, they could be individualized and synchronized as required. They were thus applicable in a society that had to include a great variety of biographies, schedules, and consequences of activity. Although they are still rituals, religious acts thereby become more compatible with a society that has become more complex.

The linear conception of time also offers advantages of an apologetic nature. From the time of Tertullian, the Church Fathers profited from the greater depth of their historical horizon. They could attain this depth by admitting dogmatic heterogeneity, namely by the in itself peculiar incorporation of the Hebraic tradition into Christian dogmatics as "Old Testament"[193]. A further consequential factor is that the Christian tradition preserves the *memory* of *prophecies* that foretold the coming of the Lord[194]. It must therefore be able to conceive a vision of the future that is located in the past. It must be able to imagine temporal determinations so that they can be applied to themselves and not just shifted chronologically. Just as the present becomes conceivable as a past of the future, especially in the idea of the Last Judgement, so also must the past be conceivable as a past present that had its own future. This latter idea becomes highly significant for the

generalization of the contingency problem in the medieval
theological   discussion   de   futuris   contingentibus.
Augustine's famous reflections in the XIth Book of the Confessions apply this temporal structure with varying horizons to any actual present and thereby set the structure
itself into historical motion[195]. The theological vola-
tility of these constructs is evident in the fact that a
dogmatics that formulates statements about time has had to
put the present truth of such statements above time[196].

These few individual considerations should dispel sim-
plistic ideas about the development of temporal experience.
It would be incorrect to assume that the Hebrews possessed,
as a sort of tribal tradition, a peculiar, namely linear,
conception of time which then, with the help of Christianity, asserted its superiority and prevailed in a kind of
cultural battle for existence. On the contrary, there were
definite religious-dogmatic interests that produced a time
problem and the necessity for a decision in the first place.
They thereby gradually and somewhat haphazardly prepared a
more complex and differentiated experience of time. Ultimately, only an abstract and linear temporal structure could
become the basis of articulation. In other words, there
seems to be a very general rule that with the increase of
analytic power in the objective dimension and the increase
of contingencies in the social sphere, the temporal dimension is ultimately the only one left that can re-establish
the conceivability of order[197].

On the other hand, a linear historicization of time
intensifies the experience of *sin*, that is, of contingent
misbehaviour. Past events must be seen within a temporal
category that is separate from the present, a category which
makes all misbehaviour irrevocable. A deed can no longer be
undone or cancelled[198]. This consciousness accompanies an

already moralized religion that interprets the contingency of behaviour in terms of a contrast between good and evil. The problem of sin is thereby shifted away from the concreteness of objective circumstances, damages, countermeasures, and sanctions into the temporal dimension. Here it is radicalized and becomes a universal problem that is the same for all human beings. Redemption can now only be conceived as the conjunction of sin and nevertheless evident grace. Here again, universalization forces a deeper understanding of the problem.

Moreover, this necessity prevents the linear idea of time from being maintained to the exclusion of all others. It is therefore misleading to speak of a linear conception of time without being more precise. It is a long time yet before time is conceived as abstractly as the modern idea, which sees time as a series of instants that is indifferent to what has happened, is happening, and will happen[199]. A salvific event that is experienced as present and an eschatology that refers to the future do not yet exclude each other even though each presupposes a different conception of time[200]. The idea of a *present* and actual (!) participation in a *past* salvific event (Romans 6:3-9) only becomes inconceivable later, namely when time, for the sake of societal co-ordination, is abstracted to the point where it becomes a linear series of instants that precludes the simultaneity of past and present events[201]. A religious conception of time cannot be compatible with every possible world. It would thereby lose its religious function of contributing to the transformation of entirely undetermined into determinable possibilities[202]. The religious conception of time refers not only to a dimension of all possibilities, but also to a real condition of possibility that is beyond earthly disposition and variation. Accordingly, the middle ages see the

relationship of eternal (without future or past), divine
presence to the changing course of time on earth not only
formally as simultaneity, but also concretely as Lordship by
means of temporal disposition[203]. By contrast, the modern
societal system exhibits an unequivocal tendency to eliminate, through standardization and abstraction of the conception of time, every limitation that stems from non-manage-
able conditions of possibility.

Probably the most decisive consequence of these changes
in the representation of time concerns their relation to the
historical development of the world and of society in particular. As long as time was more or less identified with
process or motion and only abstracted as chronology, there
were only two ways of conceiving time and the world. Either
time and the world were conceived as without beginning
(which can only mean: not conceiving a beginning) or their
beginning was sought in a generative primal cause: in a
system that is more complex than the systems it generates
because otherwise it could not generate them at all. An
explanation of the process of time and world implies the
process itself, and this self-implication, in the second
alternative, is shifted to the beginning. It is shifted
into the idea of a creative act or, if the problem is limited to the origin of structure, into the doctrine of seminal
powers as the presupposition of all development, of empeiria
as the presupposition of all learning, and of innate ideas
as the presupposition of all cognition. The beginning was,
so to speak, abandoned to paradox in order to be able to
conceive and explain the process. Moreover, faith in God as
explanatory concept and in creation obviates a decision
about   the   analytically   unsolvable   problem   of   the
beginning[204]. Corresponding modern theories have dropped
faith as a means for deciding the undecidable. These

theories include modern theories of evolution or, again, if
the problem is limited to the origin of structure, theories
about autocatalysis and the limitation of possibilities
through chance events. However, one can also do without
explanations that seek to explain processes in terms of
their beginnings. Thereby the beginning loses its dignity
(without the end gaining it as a result). The premise that
reference to a more complex system is necessary to explain
the origin of systems is superceded by the concept of
selection[205]. For science this means a painful abandonment
of explanations and prognoses for emergent developments.
Nevertheless, theories of this type have had unquestionable
success and correspond above all to the open-ended temporal
horizons in which we live today in any case.

Naturally, one glance will show that the problem of
ultimate reasons has not hereby been solved. However, this
offers small comfort to theology because questions about
ultimate reasons in the temporal dimension can no longer be
formulated in a way that will harmonize with the premises of
a creation theory.

9. A further impetus towards the construction of
dogmas may be called the *maintenance of possibility*. The
transformation of the indeterminable into the determinable
can (and must in developed societies) occur in such a way
that structure is maintained at least as the *determinate
possibility* of experience and action. The problem of the
possibility of determinacies then takes on the more
manageable form of the determinacy of possibilities.

Even the modal concept of possibility expresses a level
of generalization required by society. An example is a
level of moral expectation that must be satisfied with incom-
plete realization. Maintaining the possibility of fulfil-
ling such expectations can be interpreted as providing for

the mere possibility of religious (i.e., ascetic) *exceptional achievements and merits*. These can then be moralized
as ideal.   This is the path taken in Buddhism and in the
Christian concept of opera supererogatoria.   It presupposes
a regulative idea of scarcity that interprets the limits of
human capabilities and operates so as to create an elite:
salvation cannot be attained by everyone.   Moreover, the
maintenance of possibility can have a markedly normative
form when it is connected with the idea of God's commandments[206].   Violation of such commandments is interpreted as
sin but this does not affect the validity of the commandments.   In other words, possibility is maintained.   In the
area of soteriology, this *counter-factual* stabilitzation of
possibility requires a *mutually exclusive* opposition of
salvation and damnation, of heaven and hell.   Moreover, it
seems that supererogatory morals are more apt to produce
catalogues of achievement[207], whereas normative morals are
more apt to develop commandments and lists of sins.   The
latter therefore have peculiar difficulties with the "popular" merit theme[208].   Corresponding to the *normative*
principle is the idea that, among the conditions of salvation, *grace* receives priority over merit[209].   No matter how
the details are worked out, both primarily meritorious and
primarily normative concepts can be used to stabilize possibility.   Although the social consequences will be different
in each case, the viability of either alternative has
relatively little to do with what the particular society is
actually like.

     Aside from this basic question of the "stylization" of
expectations, individual dogmas also have a more or less
central function for the maintenance of possibility.   The
dogma of the resurrection after the frustration by the cross
interprets the experience that possibilities do not disap-

pear because of failure but rather remain preserved[210]. In the concept of the Holy Spirit, the same abstraction and independence from the concrete presence is symbolized as a kind of "installment" (not deposit!) that makes the promise binding[211]. The improbability of these events is further underscored by their uniqueness. Their significance emerges from the fact that the "Kingdom of God" was both the reason and theme for the frustrated attempt. This Kingdom triumphs in the "Resurrection." Participation in it is justification and is available to everyone. However, formulating it as an historical event obscures the mental construct that is at issue: namely that actual verification and realization are not simply tests for possibilities, but that in the frustration and the withdrawl, in the passage through negation, the possible is hardened to irrefutability. Destruction and challenges of all sorts do not mean that it is not possible[212].

Maintenance of possibility is an aspect of the maintenance of complexity, of the stabilization of a "whence" of selection. It is against this background that behaviour stands out as also possible otherwise, as action. On the basis of this stabilized complexity, society determines what is to be experienced and treated as contingent action. Religious dogmatics therefore contributes to the constitution of society as a relationship of selections. However it does this without this function becoming a theme in dogmatics itself.

10. The connection between contingency formula, symbolic medium, external differentiation concept, temporal representation, and preservation of possibility gives rise to a dogma of *revelation* in some religious traditions[213]. The dogma is an example of how the problem of reflection is handled dogmatically. It also shows how dogmas are unified

by the integrative position of certain dogmas and by making
the interpretation of any one dogma compatible with all
others. By contrast, dogmas are not unified by reference to
their common function, that is, not by reference to the
conditions of their substitutability. The dogma of revelation serves as a co-ordinating generalization. It combines
(1) a *universally available authorship* (God) with (2) *widely
applicable and interpretable contents* whose rationality and
interpretability are guaranteed, and (3) with the actual
appearance of a *possibility* in the form (4) of a *particular
historical event* which is (5) *immediately clear* because it
is particular and which (6) *cannot be changed* by any given
society because it is historically unique. Instead it is
subject only to a theological administration of dogmas.
With this conceptual discovery, dogmatics can acquire both
universal relevance and specific jurisdiction. In one
stroke, the communications medium of religion is made plausible as a symbolically generalized, communicable, and linguistic medium of interpretation. Revelation delivers and
grounds the code of the medium. At the same time, the
historical facticity of revelation creates an ever-increas-
ing pressure for abstraction. The only possible response to
this pressure is interpretation[214].

     Religions of revelation can be developed and perpet-
uated as faith religions by elaborating the meaning of what
has been revealed and of the texts that have been handed
down.   However, they cannot separate themselves entirely
from the level of cultic ritual. Precisely because of its
uniqueness, revelation needs constant repetition and a guarantee of its continual presence. Thereby rituals acquire
the new function of compensating for uniqueness. And their
relationship to the system can be interpreted with reference
to this function. This new task corresponds to their func-

tion as symbiotic mechanisms in the symbolically generalized communications medium of religion.

Finally, this key concept makes a binary form of decision possible: either yes or no. This possibility is of central significance for organizing the religious system as a church. The all-inclusive acceptance of revelation is entirely different from the mere belief in the existence of God. It constitutes entrance into a complexly organized system because it can be seen as a decision[215]. It is therefore more likely that the point of departure for formulating creeds was revelation (or the historical appearance of Christ) than the affirmation of God's existence. The Roman Church then put these creeds into a more complete and unified form so that they could be recited. Thereby they became more suitable for an organization[216]. The *possibility* of membership was therefore open to *everyone*. It depended solely on confession and not on other qualities like family membership, nationality, social status, occupation, etc. At the same time, factual membership could be demanded *regardless*[217]. The concept of revelation is compatible with socio-structural conditions that allow or even demand a universal possibility of recruitment. The conditions for such recruitment are autonomously specified by the religious system. These conditions allow a missionary politics of conversion of unbelievers that reaches beyond given societal boundaries because confession and membership are formulated so that they no longer require the individual to change his social status or his social role: the Christian can be and remain Greek *or* Roman.

The concept of revelation occupies a key position at the intersection of numerous symbolic relations and the function mediated (or hidden) by them. This position makes it reasonable *to define dogmatics itself in terms of revela-*

tion. The result is a highly generalized concept of dogma
that is, for example, independent of liturgical ritual[218].
The most functional and richly connected dogma occupies the
most favourable place in the system. It therefore becomes
determinative for the concept of dogmatics itself and can be
used not only as a code for a societal communications medium, but also as the point of reference for the formulation
of the conditions of church membership. This produces a
closed circle in which revelation is introduced as a dogma
and dogma is in turn treated as revelation—and functionally
transcending enquiries are excluded.

     11. Revelation reveals itself in that it refers to its
appearance in the world. *Theology* formulates this self-reference as the identity of God. It thereby makes use of the
fundamental self-reference of all meaning, namely, the possibility of returning to the original meaning after passing
through other meaning[219]. If theology were to arrive at a
position from which it could not return to God, one would
assume that an error had been made. That which appears to
logic or logically schematized science as error, as
tautology or petitio principii, is for theology consciously
undertaken self-reassurance, a proof of identity, or simply
paraphrasing. It is most important for theology to proceed
in such a way that the goal and premise of its argumentation
coincide; for it must in this way demonstrate that it can
make its presence felt in life. Its theoretical style is
its argument for God if it can overcome the sterility of
pure self-implication by expanding its poorly connected,
restricted language[220] without lapsing into mere metaphor or
simile. Its theoretical style is also its argument for God
if it can demonstrate the reality of God through his own
revealed self-reference.

     But some will object, saying, this will never do. The

world is too complex for this to work anymore. One can know
this and work it out with technical models. Uninterrupted
interdependencies are not repeatable. The classical ways of
breaking interdependencies, by positing a beginning and an
end (creation) or by formulating hierarchies, have been
discredited. This is precisely why theology happened upon
the expedients of sterility and metaphor and why it busies
itself combining the two. This objection gains strength if
one agrees with the assessment presented here: that the
intellectual hallmark of our time is an increasing awareness
of complexity-related problems. If this assessment is
correct, then theology will only be able to regain its
relevance in the world if it undertakes its own reductions
of complexity.

XI

More remains to be said about the potential for reflection within religious dogmatics. We may ask whether the
ability to balance these different conceptual and dogmatic
functions (namely, the institution of determinable contingency, the codification of a medium, the interpretation of
external differentiation, and the maintenance of possibility) has reached its limit in our own Christian religious
tradition; whether Christian dogmatics represents the
limiting achievement of dogmatics in general because it has
developed these functions to the point where they can just
barely be integrated. We may also ask whether this form of
dogmatics can still identify and direct a religious system
of our society. It is precisely because of its specific
achievements that the dogmatization of religion has problems
and risks. Something that has been particularly successful
can turn out to be incapable of adaptation just because it
has been so successful[221]. Dogmatics has combined religious

answers to very different kinds of social problems. It has
done this convincingly and within the religious system.
Exactly such an achievement can hinder the ability to adjust
at times of fundamental societal change. This is especially
the case when religious dogmatics, with reference to contingency formula, absorption of disappointment, medium construction, concept of differentiation, understanding of time,
etc., has to compete with very different functional equivalents and yet is restricted in its range of response to
problems by the internal requirements of the religious
system.

The same question can be asked with regard to the
strictness with which the internal/external distinction is
made. It may well be that a systemically exclusive religion
that "will have no other gods before it" excludes more abstract levels of inner religious reflection because it can
no longer be converted into a "belief." More favourable
points of departure may lie in non-exclusive religions that
have been able to combine a quasi-atheistic religion with
belief in gods of the most diverse kinds (e.g., Buddhism and
certain Hindu philosophies)[222]. However, from a sociological point of view, such a combination presupposes an
opposition between high culture and village culture[223]
which, in turn, presupposes limited communication and will
die out in this form. Sociology cannot provide a reliable
prognosis for the developmental possibilities in this
matter.

We can however still ask if the preceding analyses
cannot give cause for revising the concept of reflection.

Since ancient times and with greater frequency in
modern philosophy, the term reflection has referred to the
process of thinking. Reflection is thinking about thinking
or thinking about the participation of self in thinking.

Thinking is however only one process among many that can
become reflexive. Already in the middle ages, the theological discussion about love and will came close to other
cases of reflexivity. Beyond this, the *process* of reflexivity must not be confused with one of the possible functions of this process, namely the contingent determination
of systems[224]. A more precise analysis of the reflexive
process uses the difference between system and environment
to dissolve the simple concept of the subject as the ultimate ground (ὑποκείμενον). The discovery of the subject in
thinking is only a paradigm for something more general: that
the reflexive nature of process can change into a more radical form of systemic reflection. The reflexive process
applies itself to itself and changes itself. It therefore
does not discover itself as substance but rather as selectivity that is conditioned by the system.

A sufficiently formal understanding of this idea allows
it to be extended to all systems that conceive their own
identity with the help of reflexive processes of self-direction and that secure this identity contingently in an environment that offers other possibilities. Reflection is the
concept of perfection for the contingent system/environment
relationship. Consequently, the reflective potential of a
church cannot be measured merely by its capacity for attrac-
ting reflecting "subjects" and accommodating them within its
system[225]. More important is the form in which the contingency of its identity is brought to dogmatic determination.
Only on this basis can it attract relatively free and modern
"subjects."

In the contemporary discussion about ecclesiastical and
extra-ecclesiastical religiosity, the separation of these
two systems has been articulated primarily as an opposition
between the organization and the subject. In this distinc-

tion, reflection is expected only of the subject. The alternative is however incorrect and emphasizes questions of
membership and participation. In addition, one must consider that contingency and self-commitment in a domain that
allows choice presuppose structure. Freedom grows only with
order, not only against order. However, as such, the structures of neither psychological nor organizational systems
allow reflection at the level of selectivity possible today. For this purpose, they must not only exhibit self-crit-
ical intentionality but also adequately structured complexity[226]. Because the complexity of a new kind of global
society and its world has increased so dramatically, all
subsystems have been left with a pervasive reflection-def-
icit. This is true not only for religion, but also for
science, politics, and art. Moreover, neither an environ-
mentally conscious politics of organization nor a recom-
bination of cultural materials in subjective self-inves-
tigation is enough to make up this deficit.

     Systems theory can be used in the search for the social
conditions that would allow a solution to this problem. In
the process, systems theory itself would have to be reviewed
and revised. Usually, the relation of church and world or
of church and society is seen as a dilemma between maintenance and accommodation, as a question of greater concentration on the really central tenets of the faith or of
greater "opening up to the world." In fact, this alternative really only allows for a strategy of opting for one
direction while tolerating the other as well. Neither maintenance nor accommodation can be raised to the exclusivity
of an absolute principle. The alternative presumes a status
quo in terms of which one can plead for greater preservation
or greater openness and accommodation.

     This alternative may suffice for splitting a church

into parties. For the purposes of functionally oriented
reflection, however, it is less useful. The problem of
reflection is not comprehended within the alternative of
accommodation or non-accommodation, and especially not in
the forms of accommodation alone[227]. Instead, reflection is
related to how abstractly and distinctly systems can formulate this alternative. In any case, there is no optimal
accommodation if the environment varies very rapidly. At
most there are compromises between what would be optimal
accommodations to particular states of the environment. The
alternative of accommodation or non-accommodation is thereby
superceded by the search for dogmatic structures that
achieve both more accommodation and more maintenance at a
higher level of abstraction. These would have to be structures by which the religious system becomes more compatible
with a highly complex society and with the world that this
society both constitutes and renders determinable.

The difference between accommodation and reflection
refers to and posits a domain from which selections are
made. This difference can be specified further using the
distinction between the environment and the world. Accommodation, like influence, is a category for relations between a system and its environment. Through reflection, a
system refers itself ultimately to the world. The system
identifies itself with reference to the world without
excluding itself from the world. Accommodation changes the
structure of the system according to the mutations of the
system's environment. The system does not attribute the
environment to itself. Reflection constitutes system identity in the light of ordered possibilities for being different[228]. In the realm of accommodation, contingency appears
as dependence on....In the case of reflection, contingency
appears as a non-necessity. Within the framework of systems

theory, this distinction replaces the distinction between
chance and freedom with which German idealism formulated the
problem of contingency.

Accordingly, one might expect that reflection will
begin to direct the processes of influence and accommodation
as soon as a world relationship becomes distinct from the
environmental relationship and encompasses system-and-en-
vironment.   Internal and external then become different
modes that refer to the world of the possible.   When this
happens, it becomes necessary to formulate the unknown.

A dogmatics that holds on to the *idea of a negatable
world* in order to express rejection (inclusive of negative
experience of self) cannot approach this task because it
cannot distinguish clearly between the world and the environment[229].   In our sense of the word, reflection is blocked by
this attitude, making it possible to replace reflection with
the alternative of accommodation and rejection.   The world
cannot be negated because the act of negating presupposes
the world and constitutes it as the content of meaning.
This also means that the world cannot be transcended because
it reconstitutes itself in the very process of transcending.
It means that the references to other possibilities, which
are implied in all meaning, remain in the world: they are
the world.   Indeed, when determining the function of
religion, we started with these references to other
possibilities.

Holding on to a demiurgic, negatable concept of the
world binds religion to an other-worldly God who is actually
unimaginable.   Because of this, religion can paradoxically
base faith, in contrast to knowledge, on ultimate uniqueness
and heterogeneity.   Religion thereby differentiates faith
from the truth-medium of science[230].   As a result, faith
becomes compatible with any world whatever.   This result

must be counteracted in the thematic structures of the faith-code in problematical and incredible ways (e.g., by positing an other-worldly personality (!), God). Under these circumstances, the rules for relating the religious system and its societal environment cannot be derived from the concept of God or from the world itself. The environmental relationship of the religious system remains the same as its world relationship and therefore structurally ambivalent[231]. The dogma of revelation was tailored precisely to this problem. This dogma made it possible to believe that an over-generalized, non-worldly God could be respecified[232]. Can this dogma still fulfill its function today inasmuch as the change in the societal understanding of time has allowed it to become historical? Can revelation still adequately determine the relationship of the religious system to its environment? Can, in other words, interpretation and re-interpretation of revelation still fulfill the function of religion? Or must interpretation be replaced by reflection? These are questions which sociology can ask but not answer. Perhaps theology will be able to switch from the interpretation of revelation and the interpretation of this interpreting to reflection of interpretation that is conscious of its function.

All these considerations however only reformulate the question: How can the world of the possible be determined? This question concerns the function of religion. So long as societal systems were regional, so long as their structure was relatively concrete, so long as they had other societies as their environment, the question could be answered dogmatically. Such religious dogmatics worked with functionally unanalyzed abstractions. They were latently dependent on societal systems of the most diverse kinds and oriented themselves towards the structures of these societies (for example, stratified structures, structures of domination, morals, morally grounded contingency formulae). Above we described the secret alliance between dogmatic contents and the conditions for socio-structural compatibility. This alliance belongs to the conditions for the evolution of hitherto existing societies. Whether the global society which is being initiated today will continue to offer this possibility cannot be predicted in the transitional situation in which we find ourselves.

NOTES

[1]The most recent overview is given by Heinz Heckhausen, Bernard Weiner, "The Emergence of a Cognitive Psychology," in *New Horizons in Psychology 2*, ed. P.C. Dodwell (London, 1972), pp. 126-147.

[2]This is of course also indirectly a consequence of the use by systems theory of the internal external schema.

[3]The concept originates from research into the perception of causality and has subsequently been expanded using systems theory. The development can be reconstructed by reference to Fritz Heider, "Social Perception and Phenomenal Causality," *Psychological Review* 51 (1944), pp. 358-374; and *The Psychology of Interpersonal Relations* (New York - London, 1958); Edward E. Jones and Kenneth E. Davis, "From Acts to Disposition: The Attribution Process in Person Perception," in *Advances in Experimental Social Psychology*, ed. Leonard Berkowitz (New York - London, 1965), II, pp. 219-266; Harold H. Kelley, "Attribution Theory in Social Psychology," *Nebraska Symposium on Motivation, 1967*, pp. 192-238; Edward E. Jones et. al., *Attribution: Perceiving the Causes of Behavior* (New York, 1971).

[4]These conceptual proposals were the object of a discussion with Jürgen Habermas. See Jürgen Habermas and Niklas Luhmann, *Theorie der Gesellschaft oder Sozial-Technologie - Was Leistet die Systemforschung?* (Frankfurt, 1971), esp. pp. 75ff., 202ff., 305f.

[5]For the sub-specialty of the categorization of deviant behaviour see Peter McHugh, "A Common-Sense Conception of Deviance," in *Deviance and Respectability: The Social Construction of Moral Meanings*, ed. Jack D. Douglas (New York - London, 1970), pp. 61-88.

[6]Jürgen Habermas disputes the possibility of such an association of constitutional analysis and systems theory on principle. Cf. Habermas and Luhmann, *op. cit.*, pp. 142ff. By contrast, I see here a possibility for going beyond a theory-of-knowledge conception of the problem of constitution—for instance, beyond Max Adler, *Das Rätsel der Gesellschaft* (Vienna, 1936).

[7]Cf. Bronislaw Malinowski, *Magic, Science, and Religion and Other Essays* (Boston - Glencoe, Ill., 1948), pp. 8ff; E. Evans Pritchard, *Witchcraft, Oracles, and Magic among the Azande of the Anglo-Egyptian Sudan* (Oxford, 1937). The

common dichotomy of sacred and profane action is based on
this. In this regard, see the critical discussion of Jack
Goody, "Religion and Ritual: The Definitional Problem," *The
British Journal of Sociology* 12 (1961), pp. 142-164.

[8]Robert N. Bellah, "Religion: The Sociology of Religion," *International Encyclopedia of the Social Sciences*
(New York, 1968), XIII, pp. 406-414 (410f.), following Parsons, formulates a similar thought with the help of the
concepts of identity and subconscious motivation. Identity
is understood as "a relatively condensed, and therefore
highly general,...definition of the system *and the world*"
(underlining mine, N.L.). The systemic reference nevertheless remains unclear here, just as with subconscious motivation. Concerning the question of motivation, see also
below, pp. 64ff.

[9]In this respect it is understandable if even the
possibility of a universally applicable concept of religion
is occasionally questioned. See Werner Cohn, "Is Religion
Universal? Problems of Definition," *Journal for the Scientific Study of Religion* 3 (1962), pp. 25-33.

[10]At this point even Edmund Husserl already presupposes
some kind of constitution and therefore does not get at the
origin when he writes, "Indeterminacy, after all, necessarily means *determinability of a rigidly prescribed style*."
(*Indeen zu einer reinen Phänomenologie und phänomen-
ologischen Philosophie*, Husserliana, Vol. III (Den Haag,
1950), I, 100.

[11]For Günter Dux, "Ursprung, Funktion und Gehalt der
Religion," *Internationales Jahrbuch für Religionssoziologie*
8 (1973), 7-67, the function of religion is to bring to
expression the underlying structures of reality. It is
however not apparent how Dux himself comes to the conclusion
that what underlies reality has a (not further analyzable?)
structure.

[12]Cf. Niklas Luhmann, *Funktion der Religion* (Frankfurt,
1977), p. 18f.

[13]Similarly, Clifford Geertz, "Ethos, World-View, and
the Analysis of Sacred Symbols," *Antioch Review* 1 (1957-58),
pp. 421-237; and "Religion as Cultural System," in *Anthropological Approaches to the Study of Religion*, ed. Michael
Banton (London, 1966), pp. 1-46. Geertz sees herein a
familiar but inadequately developed theory. For the older
discussion see Albert K. Cohen, "On the Place of 'Themes'
and Kindred Concepts in Social Theory," *American Anthro-

pologist 50 (1948), pp. 436-443.   Peter L. Berger and Thomas
Luckmann, *The Social Construction of Reality: A Treatise in
the Sociology of Knowledge* (Garden City, N.Y., 1966) see
religious symbolic systems (like symbolic systems in general) somewhat more restrictedly as derivations and sediments
that result from the institutionalization and legitimation
of meaningful constructs in an already pre-constituted
world.

[14]Here lies a fine but important difference from
Parsons' view of religion. For reasons that have to do with
his systems theory, Parsons is forced to refer religion, as
a *partial* system of the social system, to a *partial*
environment with which the religious system maintains special interchange relations. He calls this part of the
environment (probably inspired by Paul Tillich, *Biblical
Religion and the Search for Ultimate Reality* (Chicago, 1955)
"ultimate reality."

[15]Let us note that systems theory has developed the
apparatus required for this only to a very limited extent.
In the following, we shall often treat the differentiation
of systems as a variable. We shall however not articulate
the resulting insights on the level of a general theory of
social systems. Instead, we will restrict ourselves to the
special case of the religious system. To a certain extent,
we do this in order to discover what effect the application
of abstract systems theory will have on research into religion. To this end, we will inquire into connections between
external and internal differentiation, generalization and
respecification, reflexivity and reflection, subsystem autonomy and media construction, as well as contingency formulae
and the themes of media-codes.

[16]Cf. Malinowski, *op. cit.*, for the one side, and
Alfred R. Radcliffe-Brown, "Taboo," in *Structure and
Function in Primitive Society* (London, 1952), pp. 133-152
(148ff.), for the other. Cf. also in this regard, George C.
Homans, "Anxiety and Ritual: The Theories of Malinowski and
Radcliffe-Brown," *American Anthropologist* 43 (1941),
pp. 164-172.

[17]In this regard, Mary Douglas, *Purity and Danger: An
Analysis of Concepts of Pollution and Taboo* (London, 1966).
Cf. also Edmund Leach, "Anthropological Aspects of Language:
Animal Categories and Verbal Abuse," in *New Directions in
the Study of Language*, ed. Eric H. Lenneberg (Cambridge,
Mass., 1964), pp. 23-63.

[18]Cf. Mary Douglas, *Natural Symbols: Explorations in*

Cosmology (London, 1970) - also for the conception of ritual
as restricted communication, discussed further on.

[19]Thus Roy A. Rappoport, "Ritual, Sanctity, and Cybernetics," *American Anthropologist* 73 (1971), pp. 59-76; and
"The Sacred in Human Evolution," *Annual Review of Ecology
and Systematics* 2 (1971), pp. 23-44; Maurice Bloch, "Symbols, Song, Dance, and Features of Articulation," *Europ-
äisches Archiv für Soziologie* 15 (1975), pp. 55-81.

[20]In this regard, Douglas, *Natural Symbols*, op. cit.

[21]Cf. below, pp. 19ff., 45ff.

[22]The origin of this special form needs a correspondingly special explanation. In the case of the Greeks, the
"re-primitivization" of an already developed culture during
the "dark ages" is most often regarded as decisive. Cf.,
for all this, especially Eric A. Havelock, *Preface to Plato*
(Cambridge, Mass., 1963).

[23]George M. Foster, "Peasant Society and the Image of
Limited Good," *American Anthropologist* 67 (1965), pp.
293-315, provides a good overview, especially in regard to
moral and institutional implications. For further development, see Niklas Luhmann, "Knappheit, Geld und die bürgerliche Gesellschaft," *Jahrbuch für Sozialwissenschaft* 23
(1972), pp. 186-210.

[24]Cf. Niklas Luhmann, "Die juristische Rechtsquellen-
lehre aus soziologischer Sicht," in *Soziologie: Sprache,
Bezug zur Sprache, Verhältnis zu anderen Wissenschaften:
René König zum 65, Geburtstag*, ed. G. Albrecht, H. Daheim,
and F. Sack (Opladen, 1973), pp. 387-399.

[25]For this, cf. Joachim Klowski, "Zum Entstehen der
logischen Argumentation," *Rheinisches Museum für Philologie*
113 (1970), pp. 111-141; and "Die Konstruktion der Begriffe
Nichts und Sein durch Parmenides," *Kant-Studien* 60 (1969),
pp. 404-416, especially from the point of view of a theory
of constitution.

[26]Aristotle, *De Interpretatione*, Chap. 12 and 13.

[27]For this and the following, cf. Melford E. Spiro,
"Religion: Problems of Definition and Explanation," in
Anthropological Approaches to the Study of Religion, ed.
Michael Banton (London, 1966), pp. 85-126; Louis Schneider,
Sociological Approach to Religion (New York, 1970), pp.
89ff; J. Milton Yinger, *The Scientific Study of Religion*

(New York, 1970), pp. 5ff. In general, analagous reservations have been expressed about the use of concepts like
complexity or contingency as typical problems for functional
analysis. See, for instance, Jürgen Habermas in Habermas
and Luhmann, *op. cit.*, pp. 146ff.; or Walter Schmidt,
"Aufklärung durch Soziologie," *Neue politische Literatur*
1971, pp. 340-354, especially p. 345f; Renate Mayntz,
"Zweckbegriff und Systemrationalität: Zu dem gleichnamigen
Buch von Niklas Luhmann," *Schmollers Jahrbuch* 91 (1971), pp.
57-63.

[28]In this regard, principally, Niklas Luhmann,
"Funktionale Methode und Systemtheorie," in *Soziologische
Aufklärung: Aufsätze zur Theorie sozialer Systeme*, 4th ed.,
I (Opladen, 1971), pp. 31-53.

[29]See the closely related attempt of Thomas F. O'Dea,
The Sociology of Religion (Englewood Cliffs, N.J., 1966),
who proceeds from the three basic problems of insecurity and
contingency, powerlessness, and scarcity. In loose connection to these, he distinguishes six functions and six
dysfunctions of religion.

[30]Paul Tillich, *Wesen und Wandel des Glaubens* (Berlin,
1961), pp. 53ff., is unclear. He claims that, although
symbols are signs which point to something else, they nevertheless participate in the reality of that to which they
refer.

[31]Spiro, *op. cit.*, p. 104f., emphasizes this point and
warns against misleading sociological formulations. Cf.
also Raymond Firth, "Problem and Assumption in the Anthropological Study of Religion," *Journal of the Royal Anthropological Institute* 89 (1959), pp. 129-148 (134f.).

[32]Concerning the function of the thematic concentration
of attention in the context of face-to-face interaction, see
Niklas Luhmann, "Einfache Sozialsysteme," in *Soziologische
Aufklärung*, II (Opladen, 1975), pp. 21-38.

[33]Cf., e.g., Paul Radin, *Primitive Man as Philosopher*
(New York, 1927); further, below, p. 34.

[34]"My own experience among the Tikopia was that I was
often asked if the spirits...were true or not, but not
whether I myself believed in them. The enquiry was to get
my opinion, not to test my allegiance. In this sense primitive religions have no dogma." (Firth, *op. cit.*, p. 137).

[35]In this regard, Kenneth Burke, *The Rhetoric of
Religion: Studies in Logology* (Boston, 1961).

[36]This use of terms may seem arbitrary. The conceptual
history of "dogma" and "dogmatics" (cf. August Deneffe,
"Dogma: Wort und Begriff," *Scholastik* 6 (1931), pp. 381-
400, 505-538; Martin Elze, "Der Begriff des Dogmas in der
Alten Kirche," *Zeitschrift für Theologie und Kirche* 61
(1964), pp. 421-438; and "Dogma," *Historisches Wörterbuch
der Philosophie* (Basel-Stuttgart, 1972), II, col. 275-277)
is in any case very changeable. One is more likely to find
earlier descriptions under the catchword, articulus fidei.

[37]This contradicts a concept of religion that tries to
treat rituals as constants—for instance, that of Anthony
F.C. Wallace, *Religion: An Anthropoligical View* (New York,
1966). For de-ritualization and its limits, see below, pp.
34ff.

[38]For this reason, Jean-Pierre Deconchy, *L'orthodoxie
religieuse: Essai de logique psycho-sociale* (Paris, 1971),
p. 116, concludes: "Finalement, dans un système de pensée à
regulation orthodoxe, il vaux toujours mieux ne rien dire.
A la limite, un orthodoxe parfait, c'est quelqu'un qui se
tait."

[39]This matter is discussed again below, p. 92f.

[40]Cf. Niklas Luhmann, *Rechtssystem und Rechtsdogmatik*
(Stuttgart, 1974).

[41]See, instead of others, Julius Kraft, "Vorfragen der
Rechtssoziologie," *Zeitschrift für vergleichende Rechtswissenschaft* 45 (1930), pp. 1-78 (29f.): "A discipline is
called dogmatics insofar as it considers certain, properly
speaking, arbitrary propositions as beyond all criticism and
therefore excludes the postulate of independent research."
Even more pointedly in *Die Unmöglichkeit der Geisteswissen-
schaft* (Leipzig, 1934), p. 38, Kraft writes, "The concept of
dogmatics contains the contradictory idea of knowledge without cognition [Erkenntnis ohne Erkenntnis]." This judgment
likely goes back to Kant but fails to appreciate the way in
which Kant (*Kritik der reinen Vernunft, Vorrede zur zweiten
Auflage*, p. xxxvf.) distinguishes dogmatics and dogmatism.

[42]For the area of law, see also the sharp distinction
in Ottmar Ballweg, *Rechtswissenschaft und Jurisprudenz*
(Basel, 1970). Erich Rothacker, "Die dogmatische Denkform
in den Geisteswissenschaften und das Problem des Histor-
ismus," *Akademie der Wissenschaft und der Literatur in*

Mainz, Abhandlungen der Geistes- und Sozialwissenschaft-
lichen Klasse 1954, No. 6, p. 257, n. 1, has a different
opinion because he sees science very generally as a conceptual task.

[43]Cf. Emile Durkheim, *De la division du travail social*
(Paris, 1893).

[44]The synopsis presented here follows Charles Ackerman
and Talcott Parsons, "The Concept of 'Social System' as a
Theoretical Device," in *Concepts, Theory, and Explanations*
in the Behavioral Sciences, ed. Gordon J. DiRenzo (New York,
1966), pp. 19-40 (36ff.).

[45]A good overview is given by Arthur O. Lovejoy, *The*
Great Chain of Being: A Study in the History of an Idea
(Cambridge, Mass., 1936). For the limits to the readiness
to accept perfection as an answer, see Martin Foss, *The Idea*
of Perfection in the Western World (Princeton, N.J., 1946)
as well as below, pp. 52ff.

[46]Cf. Martin Otswald, *Nomos and the Beginning of the*
Athenian Democracy (Oxford, 1969).

[47]In this regard and for its place in a developing
theory of communications media, more specifically, Niklas
Luhmann, "Einführende Bemerkungen zu einer Theorie generalisierter Kommunikationsmedien," in *Soziologische Aufklärung,*
II, *op. cit.,* pp. 170-192; and *Macht* (Stuttgart, 1975); and
"Ist Kunst codierbar?" in *"schön": Zur Diskussion eines*
umstrittenen Begriffs, ed. Siegfried J. Schmidt (Munich,
1976), pp. 60-95.

[48]See my article, "Wahrheit als Kommunikationsmedium,"
in Habermas and Luhmann, *Theorie der Gesellschaft,* op. cit.,
pp. 342-360.

[49]See also, Niklas Luhmann, "Knappheit, Geld und die
bürgerliche Gesellschaft," *op. cit.*

[50]Cf. Christopher Alexander, *Notes on the Synthesis*
of Form (Cambridge, Mass., 1964); Luhmann, "Ist Kunst
codierbar?" *op. cit.*

[51]Every periodization naturally brings delimitative
problems with it. We therefore only posit a very rough
distinction between archaic, culturally advanced, and modern
industrial societies. Thus also N.J. Demerath III and
Phillip E. Hammond, *Religion in Social Context: Tradition*
and Transition (New York, 1969). Robert N. Bellah, "Reli-

gious Evolution," *American Sociological Review* 29 (1964),
pp. 358-374, works with a division into five periods.

[52]In this regard, John Middleton, *Lugbara Religion:
Ritual and Authority among an East AFrican People* (London -
New York - Toronto, 1960), pp. 250ff.

[53]Cf., e.g., Jean Cazeneuve, "La connaissance d'autrui
dans les sociétés archaiques," *Cahiers Internationaux de
Sociologie* 25 (1958), pp. 75-99; A. Irving Hallowell,
"Ojibwa Ontology: Behavior and World View," in *Culture and
History: Essays in Honor of Paul Radin* (New York, 1960),
pp. 19-52; Thomas Luckmann, "On the Boundaries of the Social
World," in *Phenomenology and Social Reality: Essays in
Memory of Alfred Schutz,* ed. Maurice Natanson (Den Haag,
1970), pp. 73-100. The work of Ernst Topitsch can be read
in the same connection, above all, *Vom Ursprung und Ende der
Metaphysik* (Vienna, 1958).

[54]Thus Luckmann, *op. cit.*

[55]With regard to the evolutionarily important connection with the symbolism of political authority, Mesopotamian
and Egyptian religions seem to differ here. This is at
least what Henri Frankfort, *Kingship and the Gods* (Chicago,
1948); Talcott Parsons, *Societies: Evolutionary and Comparative Perspectives* (Englewood Cliffs, N.J., 1966), pp. 59ff.,
65; John G. Gunnell, *Political Philosophy and Time* (Middletown, Conn., 1968), pp. 34ff. assume on the basis of inadequate sources. On the other hand, see the conceptions of
the so-called Myth and Ritual School which draws more attention to cultural diffusion, above all S.H. Hooke, ed., *Myth,
Ritual, and Kingship* (Oxford, 1958), and E.O. James, *Myth
and Ritual in the Ancient Near East* (London, 1958). No
matter how one decides the controversy concerning the myths
and rituals surrounding kings, one cannot deny that even the
Egyptian religion came to a certain distancing of God and
the king and therewith to an ethic of contingent good
conduct.

[56]We are here using a specifically sociological concept
of motives that ultimately goes back to Max Weber. Cf.
below, p. 64f with further references.

[57]This understanding of the origin and function of
individuality also contradicts the predominant sociological
individualism-theory, which goes back to Durkheim, that
traces the "institutionalization of individualism" solely to
increasing differentiation of roles. Cf. Hans Gerth and C.
Wright Mills, *Character and Social Structure: The Psychol-*

ogy of Social Institutions (New York, 1953), pp. 100ff.

[58]In this regard see an interesting suggestion (but not this derivation) in Charles Drekmeier, *Kingship and Community in Early India* (Stanford, Cal., 1962), p. 289.

[59]In this regard, Gunnell, *op. cit.* pp. 39ff., Bellah, *op. cit.*, p. 367, characterizes the societal situation of the "historical religions" with the words: "The opportunity is far greater than before but so is the risk of failure." And Burr C. Brundage, "The Birth of Clio: A Résumé and Interpretation of Ancient Near Eastern Historiography," in *Teachers of History*, ed. H. Stuart Hughes (Ithaca, N.Y., 1964), pp. 199-230 (200), characterizes the view of history associated with the change with the words: "...history was written *about* kings, and not *by* kings."

[60]I follow the presentation and also the formulation of M. David, *Les dieux et le destin en Babylonie* (Paris, 1949), esp. pp. 50ff. Ms. David shows that under these conditions, the attitude towards the world of the gods motivates an orientation that connects fear and hope without unequivocal moral overtones (57ff.); and also that magical ideas are indispensible even in the framework of an advanced religion for the orchestration of rationality and will (66ff.).

[61]Here the sources allow an especially good overview of the development. Abundant illustrations of a divinity not yet fully moralized in early Israel can be found in Johannes Hempel, *Geschichten und Geschichte im Alten Testament bis zur persischen Zeit* (Gütersloh, 1964), esp. pp. 92ff. Only when the dichotomy of good and bad is posited *universally* in the *society*, i.e., when it regulates *all* action, does God also no longer have any choice but to be good.

[62]An important aspect and a kind of evolutionary hinge in this connection is the *contractual form* of communication. It presupposes control over one's own contribution. One cannot think of God as breaking a contract (cf. however the 89th Psalm!) or provide him with an exculpation because of impossibility of performance. The *contractual capacity* of the high God is therefore only conceivable in a sufficiently disciplined, hierarchically ordered divine realm. This, then, forces the development of a monotheism that, within the religious cosmos, no longer allows uncontrollable opposing forces. The religious cosmos itself is in this way "de-socialized." The freely chosen commmitment of the one God takes the place of a polytheistic divine realm which is more or less of necessity unreliable. The commandment of *faithfulness to the covenant* compels, besides remembrance of

what God has done, self-identification through conscientia
and memoria. Concerning the memoria-thesis see Johann Baptist Metz, "Politische Theologie," in *Diskussion zur "politischen Theologie"*, ed. Helmut Peukert (Mainz-Munich, 1969),
pp. 267-301 (284ff.) with further references.

[63]Thus Georg Fohrer, "Prophesie und Geschichte,"
Theologische Literaturzeitung 89 (1964), pp. 480-499   .
(498f.).

[64]See, e.g., Heinz-Dietrich Wendland, *Geschichts-
anschauung und Geschichtsbewusstsein im Neuen Testament*
(Göttingen, 1938), p. 14; James Muilenburg, "The Biblical
View of Time," *Harvard Theological Review* 53 (1961), pp.
225-252 (239ff.).

[65]Cf. for this purpose especially Hans Kelsen, *Vergelt-
ung und Kausälitat: Eine soziologische Untersuchung* (Den
Haag, 1941).

[66]This addition cannot be justified adequately with
sufficient brevity. It is based upon the fact that, in the
concept of eternity of the middle ages, the focus, doubtless
for considered reasons, is on *simultaneity* with and not
simply on merely unlimited duration! Simultaneity is however a condition aimed at the social dimension, namely a
condition of the communicative accessibility of the other.
As regards the last point, see above all Alfred Schütz, *Der
sinnhafte Aufbau der sozialen Welt: Eine Einleitung in die
verstehende Soziologie* (Vienna, 1932).

[67]Cf. for the medieval discussion especially J.M.
Parent, *La doctrine de la création dans l'école de Chartres:
Etudes et textes* (Ottawa - Paris, 1938).

[68]In this regard, see Niklas Luhmann, "Weltzeit und
Systemgeschichte," in *Soziologische Aufklärung*, II, op.
cit., pp. 103-133; and "The Future Cannot Begin," *Social
Research* 43 (1976), pp. 130-151.

[69]Cf. Lester G. Crocker, *An Age of Crisis: Man and
World in Eighteenth Century French Thought* (Baltimore,
1963); and *Nature and Culture Ethical Thought in the French
Enlightenment* (Baltimore, 1963); Roger Mercier, *La
réhabilitation de la nature humaine (1700-1750)* (Villemomble
(Seine), 1960); Günther Buck, "Selbsterhaltung und
Historizität," in *Geschichte - Ereignis und Erzählung*, ed.
Wolf-Dieter Stempel and Reinhart Koselleck (Munich, 1963),
pp. 29-94.

[70]In the sociology of religion of Schneider, *Sociological Approach.* op. cit., p. 42f., one finds a discussion and
recognition of the sociological position in this question
but its consequences for the "dogmatizability" of religions
do not come into view.

[71]As an example of an examination that pays special
attention to this see Robert N. Bellah, *Tokugawa Religion:
The Values of Pre-Industrial Japan* (Glencoe, Ill., 1957).

[72]The case most familiar to us is the Hebraic myth of
the expulsion from paradise. Another example from the
mythology of the Dinka traces the origin of scarcity to the
breaking of a prohibition because of *avarice.* Cf. Godfrey
Lienhardt, *Divinity and Experience: The Religion of the
Dinka* (Oxford, 1961) p. 33f. Comparing the two myths, the
bolder differentiation of the Hebraic myth is illuminating:
for avarice actually already presupposes scarcity. The
beginning of scarcity results from a situation that is itself already moralized by scarcity. By contrast, interest
in knowledge or curiosity is an independent motive that is
something other than scarcity. For the later history of the
curiositas theme and for its connection with modern scientific development, see Hans Blumenberg, *Die Legitimität der
Neuzeit* (Frankfurt, 1966), pp. 201ff.

[73]The political demise of the Chinese legalists because
of this question and the subsequent re-moralization of politics by the Confucians is exemplary. See especially Léon
Vandermeersch, *La formation du légisme: Recherches sur la
constitution d'une philosophie politique charactéristique de
la Chine ancienne* (Paris, 1965). S.N. Eisenstadt, *The
Political Systems of Empires* (New York - London, 1963)
offers a systematic and comparative examination of this
question. In the scientific history of early modern times,
one finds many examples of the same problem in the relation
of religion to the externally differentiated research of
truth. Cf. Robert K. Merton, "Science, Technology, and
Society in Seventeenth Century England," in *Social Theory
and Social Structure*, 2nd ed. (Glencoe, Ill., 1957); Richard
S. Westfall, *Science and Religion in Seventeenth Century
England* (New Haven, 1958). Detailed examinations show that
certain coincidences often gave research a kind of
religio-moral period of grace until it could defend itself
empirically and on the basis of its successes. See Walter
Pagel, "Religious Motives in the Medical Biology of the
Seventeenth Century," *Bulletin of the (Johns Hopkins)
Institute of the History of Medicine* 3 (1935), pp. 97-128,
213-231, 265-312. At approximately the same time and after
the spectacular discussion concerning pur amour, love was

increasingly privatized and sentimentalized. This is a
further example for a third media sphere. In this regard,
see Mercier, *op. cit.* (1960).

[74]This gives the thesis, just as unclear as it is
problematic, that religion has a primarily integrative function in society, a certain justification for this epoch of
evolution.

[75]For exact parallel problems in the early European
theory of societas civilis, see Niklas Luhmann, "Gesellschaft," in *Soziologische Aufklärung*, I, op. cit., pp.
137-153. The economically based concept of society of bourgeois society runs up against the same paradox: wanting to
conceive one part, namely the economy, as the quasi-whole.
In *both* cases, a *hierarchical* concept is offered as the
solution: in the case of the societas civilis, the concept
of political dominance, in the case of bourgeois society
(for whom dominance becomes suspect), the concepts of sub-
structure and superstructure with their current complicated
derivatives.

[76]In this regard also Schneider, *op. cit.*, pp. 14ff.
See also N. Luhmann, *Funktion der Religion*, op. cit.,
pp. 194ff., 208ff.

[77]Cf., in this regard, with illustrative details,
Hempel, *Geschichten und Geschichte*, op. cit. (1964), esp.,
pp. 76ff. The necessity of distancing oneself from success
or failure is a typical characteristic of the professional
mode of processing high societal risks. Even doctors and
priests are thereby forced into a more abstract professional
ethos.

[78]See Thomas Aquinas, *Summae Theologiae*, Ia-IIae 19,
art. 10. Cf. also Luke 14:26; Matthew 12:46-50.

[79]This differentiation of family and religion comes to
the fore quite pointedly and surprisingly in Parsonian sociology. This ascribes almost the same function of latent
pattern maintenance to the family and religion. The differentiation can, according to Parsons, therefore only signify
that the family is specialized regressively towards the
socialization of infants, while religion forms the fundamental motivational patterns of the adult. Cf. Talcott
Parsons, "Some Comments on the Pattern of Religious Organization in the United States," in *Structure and Process in
Modern Societies* (Glencoe, Ill., 1960), pp. 195-321 (302f.);
and "Mental Illness and 'Spiritual Malaise': The Role of
the Psychiatrist and of the Minister of Religion," in *Social*

Structure and Personality (New York - London, 1964), pp.
242-324 (esp. 305ff.); Robert N. Bellah, "The Place of Religion in Human Action," *Review of Religion* 22 (1958),
pp. 137-154.

[80]One can trace this *sociological* problem in Christian
dogmatics if one examines more closely what is said there
conceptually and exemplarily about love right up to the
famous discussion of pure amour.

[81]In its particulars, the analysis could and should be
substantially refined at this point. First of all, one
could add that, on the level of the societal system, vertical structures to bridge segmentary differentiation can
already be found in late archaic societies. However, there
they appear only in a form which ethnologists (at the suggestion of Aidan W. Southall, *Alur Society: A Study in
Processes and Types of Domination* [Cambridge, Eng., n.d.
(1953)]) call "pyramidal" structures *with greater power at
the base*. What is new in ecclesiastical hierarchy is that
it still bridges segmentary internal differentiation and
yet, as a hierarchy of a particular subsystem of society,
functions as a method of contact with the rest of society.
This function *pulls the greater power to the top*. That is,
the subsystem must institutionalize possibilities for giving
direction and obligations for obeying directions. This
contradiction is solved by a fundamentally unstable internal
power distribution. Furthermore, this church hierarchy
remains related to a society that integrates its own functional differentiation not only politically but also through
stratification. That is, the solidarity and permanent interests especially of the higher strata occasionally become
more important than the interests of particular political,
economic, religious, or familial roles. This is important
above all for the religious system which accommodates itself
to the society by recruiting into its own hierarchy in accor-
dance with the social strata. Finally, it is especially
important for current organizational considerations that the
traditional ecclesiastical hierarchy *is not meant to re-inte-
grate an internal, functional differentiation*. In addition,
its vertical functional differentiation is also insufficient
as long as it preserves a "pyramidal" structure which distinguishes the priest, the bishop, and the pope only as greater
or lesser exemplifications of the same species. In this
regard and for further organizational questions, see Niklas
Luhmann, "Die Organisierbarkeit von Religionen und Kirchen,"
in *Religion im Umbruch*, ed. Jakobus Wössner (Stuttgart,
1972), pp. 245-285; and *Funktion der Religion* (Frankfurt,
1977), chap. 5.

[82]Worth reading in this regard is Kenneth A. Thompson,
*Bureaucracy and Church Reform: The Organizational Response
of the Church of England to Social Change, 1800-1965*
(Oxford, 1970).

[83]Concerning the exceptional nature and relatively late
emergence of religions that understand themselves primarily
as belief, cf., for instance, A.R. Radcliffe-Brown, "Religion and Society," in *Structure and Function in Primitive
Society* (London, 1952), pp. 153-177 (155ff.); A.D. Nock,
*Conversion: The Old and the New in Religion from Alexander
the Great to Augustine of Hippo* (London, 1961) (first
edition 1933).

[84]See in this regard, for instance, Edwin O. James,
Myth and Ritual in the Ancient Near East (London, 1958),
p. 293f.

[85]Thus, e.g., Godfrey Lienhardt, *Divinity and Experi-
ence: The Religion of the Dinka* (Oxford, 1961); S.J.
Tambiah, "The Ideology of Merit and the Social Correlates of
Buddhism in a Thai Village," in *Dialectic in Practical
Religion*, ed. Edmund R. Leach (Cambridge, Eng., 1968),
pp. 41-121 (44f.).

[86]Parsons writes (in connection with a reference to the
dogma of the Trinity that does not seem to me to be entirely relevant) "...this implied, correlative with the differentiation of the church from secular society, a differentiation *within* the religious system itself, in the broadest
respect between the aspect of devotion and worship on the
one hand, and the aspect of the Christian's relation to his
fellow men on the other. The Christian community was constituted by the fact of common faith and common worship, but
the contexts in which worship was paramount were differentiated from the context of love and charity which bound the
community together in bonds of human mutuality." ("Christianity in Modern Industrial Society," in *Sociological
Theory and Modern Society* (New York - London, 1967),
pp. 385-421 (393)). In this regard also Niklas Luhmann,
Funktion der Religion, pp. 54ff.

[87]See in this regard the overview in Michael M. Ames,
"Magical-Animism and Buddhism: A Structural Analysis of the
Sinhalese Religious System," *Journal of Asian Studies* 23
(1964), pp. 21-52.

[88]In this regard also Niklas Luhmann, "Die Organisierbarkeit von Religionen und Kirchen," *op. cit.*

[89]Cf. Luhmann, *Funktion der Religion*, pp. 54ff.

[90]Concerning the cultural preparation through the Jewish prophets, see Ernst Troeltsch's well-known statements on "Gesetz der Ablösung und Verselbständigung," in *Glaube und Ethos der hebräischen Propheten*, Vol. IV of *Gesammelte Schriften* (Tübingen, 1925), pp. 34-65.

[91]Interesting in this regard but without a complete grasp of the relevant variables is Schneider, *Sociological Approach to Religion*, op. cit., pp. 73ff.

[92]In contradistinction to this, Talcott Parsons sees the significance of Christianity for the modern world primarily in the societal values, to the legitimation of which it contributed. See "Christianity," *International Encyclopedia of the Social Sciences*, Vol. II (New York, 1968), pp. 425-447.

[93]Concerning the consequences for a "political theology" today see Jürgen Moltmann, "Theologische Kritik der politischen religion," in *Kirche im Prozess der Aufklärung*, by Johann Baptist Metz, Jürgen Moltmann, and Willi Oelmüller (Munich - Mainz, 1970), pp. 11-51.

[94]*Les rites de passage* (Paris, 1909).

[95]S.G.F. Brandon, "The Origin of Religion," *The Hibbert Journal* 57 (1959), pp. 349-355, sees in these limiting cases the origin of religion in general.

[96]Cf. e.g., Morris Janowitz, *The Professional Soldier* (Glencoe, Ill., 1960), pp. 128ff. concerning initiation practices in the military academy of West Point and in general, Anselm Strauss, *Mirrors and Masks* (Glencoe, Ill., 1959), pp. 109ff.; Barney Glaser and Anselm Strauss, *Status Passage* (London, 1971).

[97]Cf. in this regard, Viktor W. Turner, "Betwixt and Between: The Liminal Period in Rites de Passage," in *Symposium on New Approaches to the Study of Religion. Proceedings of the 1964 Annual Spring Meeting of the American Ethnological Society* (Seattle, 1964), pp. 4-20.

[98]See in this regard the research into the handling of newcomers in groups and organizations, for instance, William F. Whyte, *Human Relations in the Restaurant Industry* (London - New York - Toronto, 1948), pp. 211ff.; Theodore F. Mills, *Group Structure and the Newcomer: An Experimental Study of Group Expansion* (Oslo, 1957); Peter M. Blau, "Orientation

Toward Clients in a Public Welfare Agency," *Administrative
Science Quarterly* 5 (1960), pp. 341-361 (esp. 351ff.);
Norton E. Long, "Administrative Communications," in *Concepts
and Issues in Administrative Behavior*, ed. Sidney Mailick
and Edward H. Van Noss (Englewood Cliffs, N.J., 1962), pp.
137-149; William M. Evan, "Pier Group Interaction and Organizational Socialization: A Study in Employee Turnover,"
American Sociological Review 28 (1963), pp. 436-440. The
main conclusion of this research is that the problem has
been transferred into the definition of the situation. The
problem comes to expression in paradoxical and burdensome
expectations and behaviours. For example, an unusually
formalistic behaviour is informally expected of the newcomer
and is rewarded with tolerance of mistakes; or a newcomer
takes greater exception to existing norms and yet observes
them more precisely than others, etc. There is also
parallel research into the situation, the behaviour, and the
handling of those who know of an upcoming status change, in
the extreme case, their imminent death. These people also
know that their interaction partners know about the change.
Here as well, even in the case of death, non-religious forms
of communication seem to dominate. Such communication is
conscious of the problem it is dealing with and perhaps includes religious platitudes to serve as communication aids.
Cf., for instance, Barney G. Glaser and Anselm Strauss,
Awareness of Dying (Chicago, 1965); and "Temporal Aspects of
Dying as a Non-Scheduled Status-Passage," *The American
Journal of Sociology* 71 (1965), pp. 48-59.

[99]However, here as well, the otherwise conventional,
more rational forms of stating and solving the problem press
to the fore. For example, the problem mentioned in the
previous note concerning the capacity for learning and insight also becomes acute here; and the solution to the problem by a passing rigorism or normative orientation is also
practiced here.

[100]This formula is used in connection with a functional
theory of ecclesiastical action in Karl-Wilhelm Dahm, *Beruf:
Pfarrer* (Munich, 1971), esp. pp. 116ff., 303ff. For the
second function of the "mediation of values," see below,
n. 105.

[101]"For whatever reasons" means, practically, from the
viewpoint of organization, that the cases that occur are not
predictable and that the initiative for making contact must
therefore be brought to the church from the environment.

[102]This is most noticeable in archaic societies. Cf.,
e.g., E.E. Evans-Pritchard, *Witchcraft, Oracles, and Magic*

among the Azande of the Anglo-Egyptian Sudan (Oxford, 1937); Melford E. Spiro, "Ghosts, Ifaluk, and Teleological Functionalism," *American Anthropologist* 54 (1952), pp. 497-503; Max Gluckman, *Custom and Conflict in Africa* (Oxford, 1955), pp. 81ff. For examples from the Hindu and Buddhist traditions, cf., e.g., Pauline Kolenda, "Religious Anxiety and Hindu Fate," *Journal of Asian Studies* 23 (1964), pp. 71-81; and Ames, "Magical Animism and Buddhism," *op. cit.*, esp. p. 38f. Over and above this, the key problem to which religion responds in general is often seen in this question. However, the theoretical merit of more recent sociology of religion shows itself in that this limited point of view has been overcome, superceded, and preserved in a more abstract formulation of the question that can see the absorption of disappointments and the grounding of meaning-structures as a unity. For a preliminary statement see Talcott Parsons, "The Theoretical Development of the Sociology of Religion," in *Essays in Sociological Theory*, 2nd ed. (Glencoe, Ill., 1954), pp. 197-211 (esp. 209).

[103]Concerning both these possibilities, more comprehensively, Niklas Luhmann, *Rechtssoziologie* (Reinbek, 1972), I, 40ff.

[104]Comprehensively in this regard and against the older theory of an origin of all law in religion, see A.S. Diamond, *The Evolution of Law and Order* (London, 1951). Correspondingly, Max Gluckman, "African Jurisprudence," *Advancement in Science* 18 (1962), pp. 439-454 (450f.), distinguishes between the judicial mechanism and the magical-ritual handling of disappointment.

[105]Therefore we can assign to this speical problem the second function of ecclesiastical action, which Karl-Wilhelm Dahm, *op. cit.*, pp. 116ff., 303ff., still considers immediately and practically significant for today, namely the mediation of values.

[106]Such a process can be illustrated in the medieval use of the doctrine of Anti-Christ. This doctrine presupposes a conceptual and dogmatic basis that includes an eschatological understanding of history, the notion of kingdom (cf. below, pp. 71ff.), the possibility of conceiving this notion both positively and negatively, and the ethico-political combination of this notion with doctrines of virtue and sin. This doctrine was then also applied very drastically to both societal and national events, serving to explain, intimidate, and sanction. Cf., e.g., Ernst Bernheim, *Mittelalterliche Zeitanschauungen in ihrem Einfluß auf Politik und Geschichtsschreibung* (Tübingen, 1918), I, esp. 70ff; Chris-

topher Hill, *Antichrist in Seventeenth-Century England*
(Oxford, 1971).

[107]Cf. in this regard Michel Foucault, *Psychologie und
Geisteskrankheit* (Frankfurt, 1968).   In this connection
further worth reading is Ronald D. Laing, *The Politics of
Experience* (Harmondsworth, Eng., 1967).

[108]Robert N. Bellah, "The Place of Religion in Human
Action," *Review of Religion* 22 (1958), pp. 137-154, still
makes this assumption.

[109]See "On the Concept of Value Commitments," *Sociological Inquiry* 38 (1968), pp. 135-160.   Noteworthy in this
regard, the arguments, following Parsons, of Neil J.
Smelser, *Theory of Collective Behavior* (New York, 1963)
p. 187f. about the external differentiation of religious
commitments as a presupposition of collective "crazes."
Cf. further the references above, n. 8 and 79.

[110]The general sociological use of the term essentially
does not go beyond the everyday meaning of the word.   What
is meant is as much as obligation of self, binding of self,
and these not in the sense of a natural becoming but rather
as a rejection of other possibilities.   Cf., e.g., Anselm
Strauss, *Mirrors and Masks: The Search for Identity* (Glencoe, Ill., 1959), esp. pp. 39ff.   Thornton B. Roby, "Commitment," *Behavioral Science* 5 (1960), pp. 253-264; Helen P.
Gouldner, "Dimensions of Organizational Commitment," *Administrative Science Quarterly* 4 (1960), pp. 468-490; Howard S.
Becker, "Notes on the Concept of Commitment," *American
Journal of Sociology* 66 (1960), pp. 32-40; William Korn-
hauser, "Social Bases of Political Commitment: A Study of
Liberals and Radicals," in *Human Behavior and Social Process: An Interactionist Approach*, ed. Arnold M. Rose (Boston, 1962), pp. 321-339; Rosabeth Moss Kanter, "Commitment
and Social Organization: A Study of Commitment Mechanisms
in Utopian Communities," *American Sociological Review* 33
(1968), pp. 499-517.

[111]For the conceptual history and the theological
origin of "fanaticism," see Robert Spaemann, *Reflexion und
Spontaneität: Studien über Fenelon* (Stuttgart, 1963),
pp. 163ff; and "Fanatisch," "Fanatismus," in *Historisches
Wörterbuch der Philosophie*, ed. Joachim Ritter (Basel –
Stuttgart, 1972), II, col. 904-908.

[112]Partially divergent is Talcott Parsons, "On the
Concept of Value-Commitments," *op. cit.* pp. 153ff., who
describes inflation in the area of (among others, religious)

commitments as "overcommitment," namely as more and different sorts of engagements than one can fulfill; and deflation as lack of readiness to honour commitments. Cf. also Talcott Parsons and Gerald M. Platt, *The American University* (Cambridge, Mass., 1973), pp. 304ff. For the application of the concepts inflation/deflation to the communications medium power, see David A. Baldwin, "Money and Power," *The Journal of Politics* 33 (1971), pp. 578-614 (608ff.). Further, see the attempt of Rainer C. Baum, "On Societal Media Dynamics: An Exploration," in *Explorations in the General Theory of Social Science*, ed. Jan J. Loubser, Rainer C. Baum, A. Effrat, Viktor Lidz (New York, 1976) to conceive of inflation as the too strong separation of the individual meaning-components (values, roles, norms, means) of action and deflation as too strong concentration and fusion of these meaning-components—too strong, that is, relative to the demands for compatibility with the developmental state of the society in question.

[113]Regarding the latter, Parsons, "Value-Commitments," *op. cit.*, p. 154f. with parallels to an ethnically or nationally oriented politics and to an economy bound to the gold-standard. See also Parsons, "Religion in a Modern Society," *Review of Religious Research* 7 (1966), pp. 125-146 (137ff.).

[114]Only in the case of *money* do inflation and deflation become *mutually exclusive* because of quantification and because of the principle of scarcity which is determined by the constant sum principle. This has the considerable practical advantage that one must at any given time take measures against only one or the other danger.

[115]We do not assume that this question must be decided in every religious system. Egyptian religion is a good counter-example. It includes the attempt of Ikhnaton to bring about the change to monotheism *politically*. At the same time, the failure of this attempt shows that in the 14th century B.C., neither logic (that the oneness of God would preclude the plurality of the gods) nor politics was equal to the feat. Cf. Siegfried Morenz, *Ägyptische Religion* (Stuttgart, 1960), pp. 144ff; Erik Hornung, *Der Eine und die Vielen: Ägyptische Gottesvorstellungen* (Darmstadt, 1971). (See also Bernard Delfendahl, "La multiplicité des dieux: Enquête à Kunje (Inde)," *Annales E.S.C.* 25 (1970), pp. 1523-1546.) Only in later times, after a stronger differentiation of religion and politics, could monotheism support itself on the model of the politically successful monarchy and draw from it at least plausibility and material for illustration. Interesting in this regard is Erik Peter-

son, "Der Monotheismus als politisches Problem," in *Theolog-ische Traktate* (Munich, 1951), pp. 45-147, with material that illustrates the theological danger of this modelling as well as the way towards overcoming it through the dogma of the Trinity. Cf. further, N.Q. King, "Kingship as Communi-cation and Accommodation," in *Promise and Fulfillment: Essays presented to Professor S.H. Hooke* (Edinburgh, 1963), pp. 142-162. Speaking sociologically, this political analogy is a good example of "evolutionary transitions" which, after the stabilization of an institution, must be dismantled again.

[116]An expressly evolutionary handling of precisely this theme still meets the resistance of ethnology. However, at least today it is realized that the many cases of archaic monotheism are of an entirely different sort than advanced-cultural monotheism. That is, they at least do not disprove a developmental hypothesis. In this regard, see Murray and Rosalie Wax, "Magic and Monotheism," in *Symposium on New Approaches to the Study of Religion* (Seattle, 1964), pp. 50-60; and Ralph Underhill, "Economic and Political Ante-cedents of Monotheism: A Crosscultural Study," *American Journal of Sociology* 80 (1975), pp. 841-861; further, numer-ous contributions by Raffaele Pettazzoni, for instance, *Der allwissende Gott: Zur Geschichte der Gottesidee* (Frankfurt, 1960). Theologians themselves are quite prepared to recog-nize the development of biblical monotheism. Cf., e.g., Walther Eichrodt, *Theologie des Alten Testaments*, Part I, 5th ed. (Stuttgart - Göttingen, 1957), pp. 141ff.

[117]See above, p. 26f. Besides this, see Hans Walter Wolff, "Geschichtsverständnis der alttestamentlichen Proph-etie," *Evangelische Theologie* 20 (1960), pp. 218-235; Hans Wildberger, "Jesajas Verständnis der Geschichte," *Supple-ments to Vetus Testamentum* (Leiden, 1963), IX, pp. 83-117. By contrast, under conditions prototypical for *polytheism*, the *same* process of a temporal extension of the present into the past and/or future must lead to entirely different re-sults. It leaves religion untouched. This can be shown in the often debated development of the Greek experience of time. From the extensive literature, cf. Silvio Accame, "La concezione del tempo nel' età arcaica," *Rivista di filologia e di istruzione classica*, n.s. 39 (1961), pp. 359-394; Jacqueline de Romilly, *Le temps dans la tragédie grecque* (Paris, 1971).

[118]Concerning the ingenuity of this conceptual discov-ery, cf. also Robert H. Pfeiffer, "Facts and Faith in Bibli-cal History," *Journal of Biblical Literature* 70 (1951), pp. 1-14. It made the step-by-step transition to the

universal monotheism of a universal God possible in that it
partially withdrew the generalization again by the
counter-assertion that one people was selectively preferred.
Sociologically speaking, a transfer from an ascriptive to an
achievement oriented relation of God and people is affected
thereby. This can then be developed further into a relation
between God and the individual. As regards the latter, see
Jean de Fraine, *Adam et son lignage* (Brugge, 1959).

[119]The way for this is also prepared in religions that
have not yet decided between polytheism and monotheism,
namely those that do not see an alternative here but rather,
analagous to the segmentary-pyramidal construction of the
society, see a hierarchy of religious spirits and powers
that leads to an ambivalent principle of a universal divinity. See, as examples, E.E. Evans-Pritchard, *Nuer Religion*
(Oxford, 1956); John Middleton, *Lugbara Religion* (London,
1960); E.G. Parrinder, "An African Saviour God," in *The
Saviour God: Comparative Studies in the Concept of Salvation Presented to Edwin Oliver James*, ed. S.G.F. Brandon
(Manchester, 1964), pp. 117-128, or with special emphasis on
an economy of symbols that explains "more and more in terms
of less and less" on higher levels, Robin Horton, "The
Kalabari World-View: An Outline and Interpretation," *Africa*
32 (1962), pp. 197-220 (216).

[120]Concerning the linguistic foundations for expressing
totality through dualistic oppositions, cf. Adhémar Massat,
"L'emploi en égyptien, de deux termes opposés pour exprimer
la totalité," in *Mélanges bibliques* (Festschrift André
Robert) (Paris, 1957). pp. 38-46, with further references.
Concerning the use of this possibility in archaic and high
religions, Edmund R. Leach, "Anthropological Aspects of
Language: Animal Categories and Verbal Abuse," in *New
Directions in the Study of Language*, ed. Eric H. Lenneberg
(Cambridge, Mass., 1964), pp. 23-63; and "Pulleyar and the
Lord Buddha: An Aspect of Religious Syncretism in Ceylon,"
Psychoanalysis and the Psychoanalytic Review 49 (1962),
pp. 81-102. For early Greek thinking and transitions to
logic, see G.E.R. Lloyd, *Polarity and Analogy: Two Types of
Argumentation in Early Greek Thought* (Cambridge, Eng.,
1966).

[121]Cf. *The Rhetoric of Religion*, op. cit. Further, "A
Dramatistic View of the Origins of Language," *The Quarterly
Journal of Speech* 38 (1952), pp. 252-264, 446-460, 39
(1953), pp. 79-92, 209-216 (esp. 81f.).

[122]I consciously formulate with double modalization:
necessarily non-contingent. As a parallel closer to theol-

ogy, see Henry Deku, "Possibile Logicum," *Philosophisches
Jahrbuch der Görres-Gesellschaft* 64 (1956) pp. 1-21.   Deku
traces the problem of the possibile logicum to the idea that
a supramodal necessity is necessary.

[123]This is naturally, and purely analytically for good
reasons, disputed again and again. See Ronald W. Hepburn,
*Christianity and Paradox: Critical Studies in Twentieth
Century Theology* (London, 1958); Konstantin Kolenda, "Thinking the Unthinkable: Logical Conflicts in the Traditional
Concept of God," *Journal for the Scientific Study of Religion* 8 (1969), pp. 72-78.

[124]The consequences, also sociologically important for
the interpretation of creation, sin, and the incarnation of
God, are discussed in August M. Knoll, "Thomismus und
Scotismus als Standestheologien," *Festschrift für Karl Adam*
(Düsseldorf, 1952), pp. 225-239, reprinted in *Zins und
Gnade: Studien zur Soziologie der christlichen Existenz*
(Neuwied - Berlin, 1967), pp. 5-24.

[125]In an analysis of just this consequence of perfection, Arthur Lovejoy, *The Great Chain of Being: A Study
in the History of an Idea* (repr. 1936, Cambridge, Mass.,
1950), p. 49 writes with reference to the God of Plato, "The
concept of a Self-Sufficing Perfection, by a bold logical
inversion, was—without losing any of its original implications—converted into the concept of a Self-Transcending
Fecundity."

[126]A more precise analysis could show that the actual
intellectual achievements are to be sought in a selective
combination of modalities from the theory of possibility
with epistemological, temporal, and causal modalities. For
individual aspects of these tremendously complex associa-
tions, see, e.g., Gerard Smith, "Avicenna and the Pos-
sibles," *The New Scholasticism* 17 (1943), pp. 340-357;
Thomas B. Wright, "Necessary and Contingent Being in St.
Thomas," *The New Scholasticism* 25 (1951), pp. 439-466; Guy
Jalbert, *Nécessité et contingence chez saint Thomas d'Aquin
et chez ses prédécesseurs* (Ottawa, 1961); Guy Picard,
"Matière, contingence et indéterminisme chez saint Thomas,"
Laval Theologique et Philosophique 22 (1966), pp. 197-232;
Heinrich Barth, *Philosophie der Erscheinung: Eine Problem-
geschichte*, 2nd ed. (Basel - Stuttgart, 1966), pp. 326ff.

[127]Cf. Duns Scotus, *Ordinatio I*, dist. 39, ad. arg.,
pro tertia op. "quod contingentia non est tantum privatio
vel defectus entitatis (sicut est deformitas in acto illo
qui est peccatum), immo contingentia est modus positivus

entis (sicut necessitas est alius modus), et esse positivum
—quod est in effectu—principalius est a causa priore."
Cited according to *Opera Omnia* (Civitas Vaticana, 1950ff.),
VI, 444. Cf. also Celestino Solaguren, "Contingencia y
creación en la filosophia de Duns Escoto," *Verdad y Vida* 24
(1966), pp. 55-100.

[128]See, for instance, Konstanty Michalski, "Le problème
de la volonté à Oxford et à Paris au XIVe siècle," *Studio
Philosophica* 2 (1937), pp. 233-365, reprinted in *La
Philosophie au XIVe siècle: six études* (Frankfurt, 1969);
further, very interesting sociologically as well, Léon
Baudry, *La querelle des futurs contingents (Louvain
1465-1475)* (Paris, 1950).

[129]The common handling of the opposition between
theology and the theory of evolution—e.g., Edwin O. James,
"Evolution and the Faith," *Theology* 16 (1928), pp. 2-9 -
sees the problem solely in a comparison of biblical texts,
esp. the creation story, with findings of the theory of
evolution and thus arrives at premature suggestions for
reconciliation in that it explains the biblical material as
being intended in an allegorical or merely symbolic manner.

[130]Cf. Michael Theunissen, "Ο αἰτῶν λαμβάνει: Der
Gebetsglaube Jesu und die Zeitlichkeit des Christseins," in
Jesus: Ort der Erfahrung Gottes (Frieburg - Basel - Vienna,
1976), pp. 13-68.

[131]Edward C. Dimock, Jr., *The Place of the Hidden Moon:
Erotic Mysticism in the Vaisnava-Sahajitya Cult of Bengal*
(Chicago, 1966) deals with a good example from the bhakti
movements in Hinduism. See also Dimock, Jr., "Doctrine and
Practice Among the Vaisnavas of Bengal," in *Krishna: Myths,
Rites and Attitudes*, ed. Milton Singer (Honolulu, 1966).

[132]Neoplatonic criticism drew attention to the
"misanthropicity" and the moral and political danger of this
politically anomic principle as energetically as it did
unsuccessfully. Cf., in this regard, Arnold A.T. Ehrhardt,
*Politische Metaphysik von Solon bis Augustin, Bd. III
Civitas Dei* (Tübingen, 1969), p. 2f. with further
references. Cf. also Adolf von Harnack, *Die Mission und
Ausbreitung des Christentums in den ersten drei
Jahrhunderten*, 4th ed. (Leipzig, 1924), I, 281ff. and for
further themes in this polemic, Pierre Courcelle,
"Anti-Christian Arguments and Christian Platonism: From
Ambrosius to St. Ambrose," in *The Conflict Between Paganism
and Christianity in the Fourth Century*, ed. Arnaldo
Momigliano (Oxford, 1963), pp. 151-192.

[133]Those movements also count as contingent respeci-
fications which object to generalized codes as such but
which cannot shake off the contingency of their origin and
their own selectivity. See the comments on "Fundamentalism"
by Talcott Parsons, "Religion in a Modern Society," *Review
of Religious Research* 7 (1966), pp. 125-146. The concept
therefore includes the possibility of an extra-ecclesial
constitution of sects.

[134]Cf. above, p. 47f.

[135]We shall forthwith have to qualify this statement.
See the following section on "symbiotic mechanisms"
(pp. 65ff.)

[136]This association of revelation and salvation history
as history of witnesses and interpretations is emphasized by
Oscar Cullmann, *Heil als Geschichte: Heilsgeschichtliche
Existenz im Neuen Testament* (Tübingen, 1965).

[137]We have expanded this idea in the chapter on
secularization in Niklas Luhmann, *Funktion der Religion*, *op.
cit.*, pp. 225-271, from the point of view of the external
differentiation even of complementary roles.

[138]According to this view, the dogmas themselves can be
seen as transitional stopping-places for experience which is
concerned with the matter itself. See, for instance, Thomas
Aquinas, *Summa Theologiae*, II-II, q. 1, art. 2, ad. 2:
"Actus autem credentis non terminatur ad enuntiabile, sed ad
rem: non enim formamus enuntiabilia nisi ut per ea de rebus
cognitionem habeamus, sicut in scientia, ita et in fide."
It is also noteworthy that the complexity of the mediating
symbol-structure is discussed here.

[139]Only thus (and not with the simple idea of a consensus) can it be convincingly shown that faith is possible
only as an affair of a communio, a communicating community,
and not as the correct opinion of the individual who then
occasionally casts side-glances to assure himself that
others think as he does.

[140]Concerning "formulations" in this sense, see Harold
Garfinkel and Harvey Sacks, "On Formal Structures of Politi-
cal Actions," in *Theoretical Sociology: Perspectives and
Developments*, ed. John C. McKinney and Edward A. Tiryakian
(New York, 1970), pp. 327-366.

[141]The comparison with other media may at first be
questioned by theologians. However, at least with one of

the communications media, with truth, they have always
already compared faith—see "sicut in scientia" in the above
cited Thomas quotation. The extension of the comparison is
a consequence of the theoretical and conceptual shift from
cognition to communication. This shift is a compelling
consequence of modern social scientific research.

[142]Daivd A. Baldwin, "Money and Power," *The Journal of
Politics* 33 (1971), pp. 578-614 (esp. 597ff., 605), raises
this question for the case of power.

[143]Cf. Max Weber's definition of motive in *Wirtschaft
und Gesellschaft*, 3rd ed. (Tübingen, 1948), p. 5. Since
then, see especially C. Wright Mills, "Situated Action Vocab-
ularies of Motive," *American Sociological Review* 5 (1940),
pp. 904-913; Hans Gerth and C. Wright Mills, *Person und
Gesellschaft: Die Psychologie sozialer Institutionen*
(Frankfurt - Bonn, 1970); Kenneth Burke, *A Grammar of
Motives* (Englewood Cliffs, N.J., 1945); A.R. White, "The
Language of Motives," *Mind* 67 (1958), pp. 258-263; Fritz
Heider, *The Psychology of Interpersonal Relations* (New York
- London, 1958); Alan F. Blum and Peter McHugh, "The Social
Ascription of Motives," *American Sociological Review* 36
(1971), pp. 98-109.

[144]More recent psychology is also working towards this
conception to the extent that it investigates interdependencies between the cognitive and the motivational components
of the psychological processing of information. Cf. Heckhausen and Weiner, *op. cit.* (n. 1).

[145]One of the most impressive examples of this problem
can be found in the famous/infamous moral casuistry. This
was basically a theory of motives and in this direction went
to the limits of the dogmatically justifiable. A limiting
example in the opposite direction can be seen in the theoretical speculations of the high and late middle ages about the
God-concept, omniscience, and contingency. These speculations neglected the function of religious development of
motives.

[146]Harald Weinrich, *Für eine Grammatik mit Augen und
Ohren, Handen und Füssen—am Beispiel der Präpostionen*,
Vorträge der Rheinisch-Westfälischen Akademie der Wissenschaft (Opladen, 1976), shows that linguistics can also draw
concequences from this analysis.

[147]Cf. Niklas Luhmann, "Symbiotische Mechanismen," in
Gewaltverhältnisse und die Ohnmacht der Kritik, ed. Otthein
Rammstedt (Frankfurt, 1974), pp. 107-131.

[148]Cf. Talcott Parsons, "On the Concept of Political
Power;" and "Some Reflections on the Place of Force in
Social Process," reprinted in *Sociological Theory and Modern
Society* (New York, 1967).

[149]*Natural Symbols, op. cit.*, p. 116.   Cf. also
pp. 65ff.

[150]We shall come back to this distinction below,
pp. 87ff.

[151]In this regard, Hans Wildberger, "Jesajas Verständ
nis der Geschichte," *Supplements to Vetus Testamentum*
(Leiden, 1963), IX, pp. 83-117, is worth reading.

[152]Cf. Volker Rittner, *Kulturkontakte und soziales
Lernen im Mittelalter* (Cologne - Vienna, 1973).

[153]Herein can also be found a suitable point of departure for the emergence of science. In *this* connection,
Gaston Bachelard, *La philosophie du non: Essai d'une
philosophie de nouvel-esprit scientifique*, 3rd ed. (Paris,
1962), p. 58, uses the phrase, "l'inconnu est formulé."

[154]Cf. with regard to this result, typical for
progressive differentiation, Georg Simmel, *Über soziale
Differenzierung* (Leipzig, 1890).

[155]Here would also seem to lie the system-structural
reasons, discussed by Wilhelm Kamlah, *Christentum und
Geschichtlichkeit* (Stuttgart, 1951), for that "unbounding"
or "un-limiting" of the idea of history by the prophets of
Israel.

[156]Augustine, *Civitas Dei*, I, 25.

[157]"Was ist 'Welt' in der Geschichte?" *Saeculum* 6
(1955), pp. 1-9 (3).   Concerning the same question, see
Köhler, "Versuch, Kategorien der Welt zu bestimmen,"
Saeculum 9 (1958), pp. 446-457.

[158]Concerning the relative independence of religion and
social structure in earlier societies, cf. also Raymond
Firth, "Problem and Assumption in an Anthropological Study
of Religion," *The Journal of the Royal Anthropological
Institute* 89 (1959), pp. 129-148 (140ff.)

[159]Conversely, the concept opposite to the civitas Dei,
Augustine's civitas terrena, cannot be understood merely as
the politically constituted society. Generally speaking,

the opposition of civitas Dei and civitas terrena in
Augustine is formulated in such a multifaceted (and in many
respects, contradictory) way that it excluded a unitary,
theocratic solution in spite of the built-in bias. It
demanded only that politics be compatible with the Christian
faith.

[160]Proofs are in Arnold A.T. Ehrhardt, *Politische
Metaphysik von Solon bis Augustin*, 3 Vols. (Tübingen,
1959-1969), esp. Vol. II.

[161]Theologians (Moltmann, "Theologische Kritik," *op.
cit.* (see n. 93), p. 27, following Peterson) as well as
sociologists (Parsons, "Christianity and the Modern
Industrial Society," *op. cit.* (see n. 86), p. 393) see this
association.

[162]The relation of the "Kingdom of God" and the
"church" is interpreted here as a relation of system and
externally differentiated subsystem and not, as it often is
(e.g., Wolfhart Pannenberg, *Thesen zur Theologie der Kirche*
(Munich, 1971), p. 9) as a relation of means and end.

[163]I have already drawn attention to the significance
of this question for the self-determination of societal
subsystems above, p. 30f. and n. 75.

[164]Cf. in this regard, and for further dualities,
Yorick Spiegel, *Kirche als bürokratische Organisation*
(Munich, 1969), pp. 78ff., following Wolf-Dieter Marsch,
"Kirche als Institution in der Gesellschaft," *Zeitschrift
für evangelische Ethik* 4 (1960), pp. 73-92.

[165]Concerning the following, see the more detailed
treatment in Niklas Luhmann, "Die Organisierbarkeit von
Religionen und Kirchen," *op. cit.* (see n. 81); further,
Funktion der Religion, op. cit. (n. 81), chap. 5.

[166]In this regard, Niklas Luhmann, *Politische Planung:
Aufsätze zur Soziologie von Politik und Verwaltung* (Opladen,
1971), esp. pp. 66ff., 165ff.

[167]Cf. Luhmann, *Soziologische Aufklärung*, I, *op. cit.*
(see n. 28), pp. 204ff.

[168]*Ibid.*, pp. 232ff.

[169]Cf. above, p. 40f.

[170]Cf. in this regard, Gananath Obeyesekere, "Theodicy,

Sin, and Salvation in the Sociology of Buddhism," in *Dialectic in Practical Religion*, ed. Edmund R. Leach (Cambridge, Eng., 1968), pp. 7-40 (12ff.), with the important reference to the difference it makes in *this* question as to whether the reincarnation theme is adopted from archaic traditions or not.

[171]Both forms of dealing with the problem are still evident in India. See Christoph von Fürer-Haimendorf, "The After-Life in Indian Tribal Belief," *The Journal of the Royal Anthropological Institute* 83 (1953), pp. 37-49.

[172]This however in very different ways and with very different degrees of concentration on the topic of salvation. S.G.F. Brandon, ed., *The Saviour God: Comparative Studies in the Concept of Salvation Presented to Edwin Oliver James* (Manchester, 1963), provides an overview.

[173]Schneider, *Sociological Approach*, op. cit. (see n. 27), p. 127, speaks of "soteriological pressure." A good overview of the question can be found here, pp. 123-153.

[174]Cf. Luhmann, *Funktion der Religion*, op. cit. (see n. 81), pp. 54ff.

[175]See the comprehensive treatment of Otto Hermann Pesch, *Theologie der Rechtfertigung bei Martin Luther und Thomas von Aquin* (Mainz, 1967).

[176]I draw attention to the fact that the *contributions* of dogmatics to *systematization* come into play here. Other illustrations for this are that the certainty of salvation is based on *revelation*, and that the acquisition of faith, that is, recognition of the specifically religious medium-code, is treated as a factor of salvation—all in all, therefore, a game with very few figures.

[177]For the most recent state of this discussion, see Shmuel N. Eisenstadt, ed., *The Protestant Ethic and Modernization: A Comparative View* (New York, 1968).

[178]Cf. Werner Dettloff, *Die Lehre von der acceptatio divina bei Johannes Duns Scotus mit besonderer Berücksichtigung der Rechtfertigungslehre* (Werl, 1954); and *Die Entwicklung der Akzeptations- und Verdienstlehre von Duns Scotus bis Luther mit besonderer Berücksichtigung der Franziskanertheologen* (Munster, 1963).

[179]Cf. Aloysius Spindler, *Cur Verbum caro factum?* (Paderborn, 1938).

[180]A bit simplified, but in principle with justice,
August M. Knoll, "Thomismus und Scotismus als Standestheologien," *op. cit.* (see n. 124), sees the reasons and
consequences of this controversy in a respectively more
ecclesiastical and more world-related orientation.

[181]Cf., e.g., the sources examined by Walter Freund,
Modernus und andere Zeitbegriffe des Mittelalters (Cologne –
Graz, 1957), from the 5th/6th to the 12th centuries A.D.

[182]This is also and especially valid for the distinction of different world ages. In this regard, Auguste
Luneau, *L'histoire du salut chez les Pères de l'Eglise: La
doctrine des âges du monde* (Paris, 1964).

[183]Cf., as an example from a very extensive literature,
James Muilenberg, "The Biblical View of Time," *Harvard
Theological Review* 54 (1961), pp. 225-252 (esp. 246ff.)

[184]Cf. Karl Lowith, *Weltgeschichte und Heilsgeschehen:
Die Theologischen Voraussetzungen der Geschichts-
philosophie*, 2nd ed. (Stuttgart, 1953), pp. 168ff.

[185]Cf. Siegfried Morenz, *Ägyptische Religion*, 2nd ed.
(Stuttgart, 1960), pp. 79ff.

[186]Oscar Cullmann's presentation is probably the most
familiar. See *Christus und die Zeit: Die urchristliche
Zeit- und Geschichtsauffassung* (Zollikon – Zurich, 1946),
esp. pp. 43ff.

[187]In this regard, comprehensively, James Barr, *Biblical Words for Time* (London, 1962). Just as critical,
Arnaldo Momigliano, "Time in Ancient Historiography," and
Chester G. Starr, "Historical and Philosophical Time," both
in *History and the Concept of Time*, Supplement 6 of History
and Theory (n.p. [Middletown, Conn.], 1966), pp. 1-23, and
24-35. Besides these, see Pierre Vidal-Naquet, "Temps de
dieux et temps des hommes: Essai sur quelques aspects de
l'experience temporelle chez les Grecs," *Revue de l'histoire
des religions* 157 (1960), pp. 55-80; Norman H. Snaith, "Time
in the Old Testament," in *Promise and Fulfillment: Essays
Presented to Professor S.H. Hooke* (Edinburgh, 1963), pp.
175-186; Thorleif Boman, *Das hebräishce Denken im Vergleich
mit dem Griechischen*, 3rd ed. (Gottingen, 1959), pp. 114ff.,
140ff.

[188]Cf. Cullmann, *op. cit.* (n. 186), pp. 107ff.
Attempts to sacrifice this uniqueness of the salvific event
for the sake of the concept of time show how difficult it

was, even here, to turn *against* the cyclical idea of time
while opting *for* the linear concept of time. Cf.
Henri-Charles Puech, "La Gnose et le temps," *Eranos-Jahrbuch*
20 (1951), pp. 57-113 (70ff.) with further references. In
the middle ages, precisely this problem of linearity is
still solved cyclically - see Georges Poulet, *Les
metamorphoses du cercle (Paris, 1961); Max Seckler, Das Heil
in der Geschichte: Geschichtstheologisches Denken bei
Thomas von Aquin* (Munich, 1964)—and the picture of a circle
of time serves to distinguish earthly time from the centre
of the circle, the divine present, which is contemporary
with all times.

     [189]Cf. Augustine, *Civitas Dei*, XII, Chap. 14—it would
be interesting to compare the late antique state of the
question with the early modern discussion of the plurality
of worlds, a discussion which raised the same problem (does
every world have its Eve, its serpent, its apple?) but which
evidently aroused much less theological opposition. The
assumption of a plurality of worlds in modern times at least
did not founder on its theological implications.

     [190]Its improbability is not only discernible in the
ridicule and rejection with which it was first received in
heathen antiquity, but also in that it was not possible to
implement it completely in popular religion. Concerning the
corrective of the wide-spread belief in "Heavenly Letters,"
cf. R. Stübe, *Der Himmelsbrief: Ein Beitrag zur allgemeinen
Religionsgeschichte* (Tübingen, 1918).

     [191]That even in such cults reference was already made
to unique events of the past—cf. S.G.F. Brandon, *History,
Time, and Deity* (Manchester - New York, 1965), pp. 71ff.—
demonstrates anew that for older epochs, it is simply not
possible to presume an option between linear and cyclical
time. See also Brandon, "The Myth and Ritual Position
Critically Examined," in *Myth, Ritual, and Kingship*, ed.
S.H. Hooke (Oxford, 1958), pp. 261-291 (284ff.), concerning
the juxtaposition of Yahweh-theology and common oriental,
cyclically oriented ritual.

     [192]and are to this extent successors of a mythical
ritual that was not yet conceived as "celebration" or as
"remembrance" of a past event, but rather as immediate repetition according to an accredited pattern. In this regard,
with plentiful material, Konrad Theodor Preuss, *Der religiöse Gehalt der Mythen* (Tübingen, 1933). Concerning the
history-of-dogma reasons for changing this concept through
the memoria-thesis, cf. also above, n. 62. Further, Brevard
S. Childs, *Memory and Tradition in Israel* (London, 1962),

pp. 74ff., 81ff., and concerning variations in Greek
thought, Paula Philippson, *Untersuchungen uber den griechischen Mythos* (Zurich, 1944).

[193]It is doubtful if they made a great impression on
the heathen world thereby. Cf. Momigliano, *op. cit.* (see
n. 187), p. 21f.

[194]This also involves a commitment to an essentially
predictable future of in themselves fixed events and therefore acts as an important *restriction* on temporal complexity. However, in late classical antiquity, this was nothing
special. This age after all believed in divination on the
basis of present (!) and obscure signs with nevertheless
fixed meanings.

[195]Cf., esp. *Confessions*, XI, 23-26. It is also
noteworthy that even here the linear course of time must not
necessarily be conceived as opposite to the cyclical model;
and that even the archaic distinction between near time and
distant time, which distinction precedes both the cyclical
and linear rationalizations, is preserved in the words, "sed
ex aliquo procedit occulto, cum ex futuro fit praesens, et
in aliquod recedit occultum, cum ex praesenti fit
praeteritum" (*Conf.* XI, 22). Cf., concerning this idea of a
distant time that no longer separates future and past, also
Ernst Jenni, *Das Wort "ōlam" im Alten Testament* (Berlin,
1953). Correspondingly, concerning the origin of αἰων, A.P.
Orbán, *Les dénominations du monde chez les premiers
chrétiens* (Nijmegen, 1970), pp. 97ff., and from ethnological
research, e.g., John Nbiti, "Les Africains et la notion du
temps," *Africa* 8:22 (1967), pp. 33-41. Even that which
Augustine experiences as the most intense introspection and
searching of conscience reproduces and recombines linguistic
and cultural patterns.

[196]Concerning the logical problems, cf. Arthur N.
Prior, "The Formalities of Omniscience," in *Papers on Time
and Tense* (Oxford, 1968), pp. 26-44; concerning the
connected problem of a *theological* history of the church,
cf. the overview of Peter Meinhold, "Weltgeschichte -
Kirchengeschichte - Heilsgeschichte," *Saeculum* 9 (1958),
pp. 261-281.

[197]See in this regard the interpretation of Kantian
natural history and theory of the heavens in Hans Blumenberg, *Die Genesis der kopernikanischen Welt* (Frankfurt,
1975), pp. 66ff.

[198]Cf., in this regard, the chapters about "Time and

Guilt" and about "Atonement" in Josiah Royce, *The Problem of
Christianity* (New York, 1913; repr. Chicago - London, 1968),
pp. 143ff. The same problem of irretrievable passing away
comes up in another form in the Greek tragedies. In this
regard, see (while working out the opposite of the cyclical
concept of time) Victor Goldschmidt, "Le problème de la
tragédie d'après Platon," *Revue des Etudes Grecques* (1948),
pp. 19-44 (57f).

[199]See also the reservations of John G. Gunnell,
Political Philosophy and Time (Middletown, Conn., 1968),
p. 63f.

[200]As the current discussion of this question mostly
assumes. In this regard, see an opposing opinion in Werner
Georg Kümmel, "Futuristische und präsentische Eschatologie
im ältesten Christentum," *New Testament Studies* 5 (1959),
pp. 113-126; and *Verheißung und Erfüllung: Untersuchungen
zur Eschatologischen Verkündigung Jesu* (Basel, 1945); and
for the Old Testament, Walter Eichrodt, "Heilserfahrung und
Zeitverständnis im Alten Testament," *Theologische Zeitschrift* 12 (1956), pp. 103-125.

[201]Conversely, *this* conception of time calls for a
complete neutralization of *past* misbehaviour in so far as it
does not bring with it future consequences and problems—
that is, a switch from punishment for wrong-doing to punishment for the sake of prevention.

[202]In modern historicism, the "final religion of the
intelligentsia" (Croce), world history itself takes over the
function of the guarantee of determinability. Cf. in this
regard, Karl Löwith, "Christentum und Geschichte," *Numen* 2
(1955), pp. 147-155. In the meantime, the question of
"world history and salvation history" is put into question
by the rudiments of an evolutionary theory of origins which
no longer sees the "laws of evolution" as the principle of
historical development, but rather sees a combination of
mechanisms that are able to produce an infinitely complex
world of determinable states. In this theory, the analysis
of the self-selection of being takes the place of religion.

[203]See, as a clear example, the text from the Boethius
glosses of William of Conches printed in J.M. Parent, *La
doctrine de la création dans l'école de Chartres: Etudes et
textes* (Paris - Ottawa, 1938), pp. 124ff.

[204]Cf. Anton Antweiler, *Die Anfanglosigkeit der Welt
nach Thomas von Aquin und Kant* (Trier, n.d. [1961]).

205For an explicit discussion of this point see Robert B.
Glassman, "Selection Processes in Living Systems: Role in Cog-
nitive Construction and Recovery from Brain Damage," *Behavioral
Science* 19 (1974), pp. 149-165.

206Anglo-Saxon writers have recently discussed if and how
marked normativity and the concept of supererogatory achieve-
ments can be compatible in commandments and duties. Cf., e.g.,
Joel Feinberg, "Supererogation and Rules," *Ethics* 71 (1961),
pp. 276-288, reprinted in Feinberg, *Doing and Deserving: Essays
in the Theory of Responsibility* (Princeton, 1970), pp. 3-24;
Roderick M. Chisholm, "Supererogation and Offence: A Conceptual
Scheme for Ethics," *Ratio* 5 (1963), pp. 1-14; Michael Stocker,
"Supererogation and Rules," in *Studies in Moral Philosophy*,
American Philosophical Quarterly, Monograph No. 1 (Oxford, 1968),
pp. 53-63.   These studies have, as yet at least, not produced an
extremely convincing possibility for a *unified* moral theory that
includes *both* forms of moralization. They have also had difficulty
in defining their logical extension.   In this situation, one can
understand why Christian theology, with its primarily normative
orientation, could only include the possibility of *supplementary*
supererogatory merits.   This combination has, in effect, weakened
the elite-creating tendencies of a purely supererogatory morals
and brought about a situation in which the cleric is also interested in the
salvation of the lay people.

207Cf. in this regard, Christoph von Fürer-Haimendorf,
Morals and Merit (London, 1967); S.J. Tambiah, "The Ideology of
Merit and the Social Correlates of Buddhism in a Thai Village,"
in *Buddhism and the Spirit Cults in North-Eastern Thailand*, ed.
Edmund R. Leach (Cambridge, Eng., 1970), p. 147; J.A.N. Mulder,
"Merit: An Investigation of the Motivational Qualities of the
Buddhist Concept of Merit in Thailand," *Social Compass* 16 (1969),
pp. 109-120.

208Which are well illustrated by the problem of whether and
to what extent merits can be earned for the sake of others regardless of their sinfulness and state of grace.   See in this
regard, the overview of Johannes Czerny, *Das übernaturliche
Verdienst fur andere: Eine Untersuchung uber die Entwicklung
dieser Lehre von der Frühscholastik an bis zur Theologie der
Gegenwart* (Freiburg, Switz., 1957).   For a comparison of the
Buddhist and Christian ideas of merit, see Ninian Smart, "The Work
of Christ," in *The Saviour God: Comparative Studies in the
Concept of Salvation Presented to Edwin Oliver James*, ed. S.G.F.
Brandon (Manchester, 1963), pp. 160-173.   Smart contrasts the two
as pragmatic and historical respectively.   This could be connected
with the fact that the normative overall view of Christianity did
not allow a completely individualized pragmatism and therefore
had to conceive action historically.

[209]The *de-individualization* of the suffering of Christ
necessary for this is noteworthy—see Thomas Aquinas, *Summa
Theologiae*, III, q. 48, art. 1: "Christo data est gratia
non solum singulari personae, sed inquantum est caput
Ecclesiae, ut scilicet ab ipso redundaret ad membra" as
answer to the express question concerning the merit-value of
the Passion. It is in any case wrong to equate this theoretical distinction between normative-obligatory and meritorious (supererogatory) aspects with a distinction between
juridical and ethical merit as is done from time to time in
the German literature. See, e.g., Hans Dombois,
"Juristische Bemerkungen zur Satisfaktionslehre des Anselm
von Canterbury," *Neue Zeitschrift für Systematische
Theologie und Religionsphilosophie* 9 (1967), pp. 339-355;
Hans Kessler, *Die theologische Bedeutung des Todes Jesu:
Eine traditionsgeschichtliche Untersuchung* (Düsseldorf,
1970), pp. 188ff.

[210]Cf. in this regard, from the theological side, the
interpretation of the death and resurrection of Christ as
passage through nothingness and thereby revelation of a
possibility that can no longer be conceived as conditioned
by reality in Eberhard Jüngel, "Die Welt als Möglichkeit und
Wirklichkeit," *Evangelische Theologie* 29 (1969),
pp. 417-422.

[211]2 Cor. 1:22.

[212]I thank Friedrich Rudolf Hohl for this idea.

[213]The evolutionarily important continuity with earlier
forms of magical religiosity, for instance, the experiencing
and witnessing of inspiration, incarnation, or prophecy, can
be seen particularly well in this concept. In other respects, this continuity could compensate for discontinu-
ities, especially the transition to monotheism.

[214]The stress and strain on the religious system that
results from this can be discerned in counter-institutions,
for instance in the already mentioned "Heavenly Letters"
which were revered as proclamations of divine knowledge and
will in the present.

[215]A.D. Nock, *Conversion* (London, 1961), particularly
emphasizes the cultural novelty of this syndrome of individual decision-making as a resort to a new kind of piety,
entrance into the system, and acceptance of an elaborated
faith-code. The genetic situation, in which the religious
communications medium had to be articulated primarily for
entrance decisions, had a continuing effect on the inter-

relations between faith and church, between medium and organized system. Out of the boundary situations of conversion
and heresy, a kind of medium-code is developed that, as
religion, possibly demands too much.

[216]There are two assumptions here. One is that affin-
ity of a religious system for organization is connected with
dogmatic contents. The other is that meanings change in a
communications medium that claims to be relevant for the
entire society if the code is used for the purposes of organizations. In the case of creeds, these assumptions need to
be examined further with modern theoretical tools. Hans
Lietzmann, "Die Anfänge des Glaubensbekenntnisses," *Festgabe
Adolf von Harnack* (Tübingen, 1921), pp. 226-242, attempted
to prove the existence of an independent and special "Christ-
ological" creed. See in addition, Oscar Cullmann, *Die
ersten christlichen Glaubensbekenntnisse* (Zollikon - Zurich,
1943). Further, concerning the emergence of a syndrome of
creed and organization, Arnold Ehrhardt, "Christianity
before the Apostles' Creed," *Harvard Theological Review* 55
(1962), pp. 73-119, who follows Walter Bauer, *Recht-
gläubigkeit und Ketzerei im ältesten Christentum* (Tübingen,
1934).

[217]It is a familiar socio-historical phenomenon that
different social groups become relevant for religious systems that go this way than for a politics ordered according
to territory and social strata; and that conflicts between
religion and politics are a result. Cf., in this regard,
S.N. Eisenstadt, "Religious Organizations and Political
Process," *Journal of Asian Studies* 21 (1962), pp. 271-294;
and *The Political Systems of Empires* (New York - London,
1963), pp. 62ff; Schneider, *Sociological Approach, op. cit.*
(see n. 27), pp. 73ff; Talcott Parsons, *The System of Modern
Societies* (Englewood Cliffs, N.J., 1971), pp. 30ff. This
tendency towards abstraction of the societal reference
through separation from kinship or territorially constituted
affinities is reflected in Christian dogmatics in the
already discussed "Kingdom of God."

[218]As a careful qualification of this specifically
modern understanding of dogma, one which peaked at Vatican
I, cf., for instance, Walter Kasper, "Geschichtlichkeit der
Dogmen?" *Stimmen der Zeit* 179 (1967), pp. 401-416.

[219]Cf. Luhmann, *Funktion der Religion, op. cit.* (see n.
81), Chap. 1, III.

[220]In this regard, Pierre Deconchy, *L'orthodoxie
religieuse* (Paris, 1971).

[221]Cf. the concept of "obstacle épistémologique" in
Gaston Bachelard, *La formation de l'esprit scientifique*
(Paris, 1947), a concept tailored to the science system.   It
designates an insufficient integration, relative to the
state of development, of ideas in the life-world.

[222]Cf. Gananath Obeyesekere, "The Great Tradition and
the Little Tradition in the Perspective of Sinhalese Buddhism," *Journal of Asian Studies* 22 (1963), pp. 139-153; and
"Theodicy, Sin, and Salvation in a Sociology of Buddhism,"
in *Dialectic in Practical Religion*, ed. Edmund R. Leach
(Cambridge, Eng., 1968), pp. 7-40; further, the contribu-
tions of Tambiah and Robinson in the same volume; Georges
Condominas, "Notes sur le Bouddhism populaire en milieu
rural de Lao," *Archives de sociologie des religions* 25
(1968), pp. 81-110, 26 (1968), pp. 111-150; S.J. Tambiah,
Buddhism and Spirit Cults in North-Eastern Thailand
(Cambridge, Eng., 1970); Richard F. Gombrich, *Precept and
Practice: Traditional Buddhism in the Rural Highlands of
Ceylon* (Oxford, 1971).

[223]Cf. Robert Redfield, *Peasant Society and Culture*
(Chicago, 1956).

[224]Cf. Niklas Luhmann, "Reflexive Mechanismen," in
Soziologische Aufklärung, I, *op. cit.* (see n. 27),
pp. 92ff.

[225]Cf. Helmut Schelsky, "Ist Dauerreflexion insti-
tutionalisierbar?" *Zeitschrift für evangelische Ethik* 1
(1957), pp. 153-174, reprinted in Schelsky, *Auf der Suche
nach Wirklichkeit: Gesammelte Aufsätze* (Düsseldorf -
Cologne, 1965), pp. 250-275.   I could accept the results of
the ideas for demarcating sociology and theology developed
by Schelsky in this connection (see Schelsky, "Religionssoziologie und Theologie," *Zeitschrift für evangelische
Ethik* 3 (1959), pp. 129-145).   However, I do not see the
distinguishing factor primarily in the position taken with
regard to the problem of values, but rather in the difference of the communications media, truth and faith, and,
connected with this, in the degree of abstraction of theo-
retically admissible research strategies.

[226]Franz-Xavier Kaufmann, "Kirliche und
ausserkirchliche Religiosität," in *Theologie in
soziologischer Sicht* (Freiburg, 1973), pp. 93-126, draws
attention to the fact that this thesis could promote an
elitist understanding of religion.   In fact, the problem
consists in the extent to which the necessary differentiation of levels must be reinforced by differentiation of

roles. And this becomes all the more likely if one persists
in defining reflection as a characteristic of the individual
subject.

[227]Naturally, this does not exclude the possibility of
also meaningfully examining the forms in which religions
could accommodate themselves to modern circumstances. See
from the extensive literature, e.g., Michael M. Ames, "The
Impact of Western Education on Religion and Society in
Ceylon," *Pacific Affairs* 40 (1967), pp. 19-42; Monica
Wilson, *Religion and Transformation in Society* (Cambridge,
Eng., 1971); François Houtart, "Les fonctions sociales de la
symbolique religieuse chez les Bouddhistes à Sri Lanka,"
Archives des Sciences Sociales des Religions 37 (1974),
pp. 23-41.

[228]Hegel, *Wissenschaft der Logik*, ed. Lasson (Leipzig,
1934), II, pp. 169ff., as is familiar, attempted to conceive
this modalization of internal and external as a "dialectic"
movement and thereby shifted the problem of reflection into
the temporal dimension.

[229]Cf. above, p. 70f.

[230]Cf. above p. 61.

[231]Cf. above, p. 69f.

[232]Cf. above, pp. 89ff.